Rabbits Everywhere

Rabbits Everywhere

by Alicia Ezpeleta

HARRY N. ABRAMS, INC., PUBLISHERS

Editor: Harriet Whelchel

Designer: Carol Robson

Photo Editor: Uta Hoffmann

Library of Congress Cataloging-in-Publication Data

Ezpeleta, Alicia
     Rabbits everywhere/by Alicia Ezpeleta.
          p.   cm.
     Includes bibliographical references and index.
     ISBN 0–8109–3781–6 (hardcover)
     1. Rabbits in art.   2. Arts.   I. Title.
NX650.R33E96   1996
704.9′432—dc20   95–620

Endpapers:
Bunny Pasta™. FunFoods, Inc.,
Hoboken, New Jersey

Pages 2–3:
Satoshi Yabuuchi. *Hare Leaping over
Moon.* 1992. Japanese cypress, lacquer,
powder paint, gold; height 18⅞".
Private Collection

Contents

"Down the Rabbit Hole" 12

"What's Up, Doc?": Rabbits as Symbols 20

Fertility and Sexuality 30
Vitality and Immortality 38
Speed and Cunning 44
Fear and Cowardice 50

"Let's Have Different Colored Rabbits, George": Rabbits in Art 56

Pastoral Rabbits 68
Literary Rabbits 84
Decorative Rabbits 90

"Stay Away from Mr. McGregor's Garden":
Rabbits in the World of Children 108

Selected Bibliography 125

Index 126

Photograph Credits 128

Acknowledgments 128

To my dear daughter
Paula,
with much love

Opposite:
Detail of *Sense of Taste*. Brussels (Franco-Flemish), c. 1480–1500. Tapestry. Musée de Cluny, Paris

Pages 8–9: Collection of buttons depicting rabbits. 18th–20th century. Various countries and materials, diameter of largest button 1¾″. Collection of Diana Epstein and Millicent Safro, Tender Buttons, New York

Jennifer Bartlett. *11 A.M., Bull Shirt*, 1992–93. Oil and silkscreen on canvas, 3'6" x 5'. Private Collection, Courtesy Paula Cooper Gallery, New York

"Tell me—like you done before."
"Tell you what?"
"About the rabbits."
—John Steinbeck, OF MICE AND MEN

Clever, foolish; brave, cowardly; cute, frightening; chaste, sexual—throughout history, rabbits have represented almost every emotion, ideal, foible, and personality trait known to humanity. In China, for example, the rabbit is a symbol of eternal life and good fortune, but to call a man a *t'u-tze* ("rabbit" or "hare" in Chinese) is a gross insult.

Various biological differences exist between rabbits and hares; rabbits have shorter hind legs and ears and are usually lighter in color than hares. For the purposes of this book, however, the terms will be essentially interchangeable. In fact, in many cultures, no distinction is made between these animals.

At some point, almost every culture has included rabbits in its folkloric, literary, and artistic traditions. Rabbits have been recorded in art since ancient times, often merely as decorative elements or examples of nature illustrations; at other times, however, they are powerful symbols. Egyptians used a rabbit hieroglyph and decorated the walls of their tombs with images of the animal.

Opposite:
The Animals in Council. From an Answar-i-Suhayli manuscript. India, 1354. Add.18579, folio146r. By permission of the British Library, Oriental and India Office Collections, London

Right:
Hare amulet. Egypt, Ptolomaic Period, 330–304 B.C. Faience, length 1⅜". Rogers Fund, 1944. The Metropolitan Museum of Art, New York. 44.4.25

Decorative rabbits were embroidered into Coptic tunics; they appear again on Roman coins, Japanese screens, Anglo-Saxon illuminations, medieval tapestries, Renaissance studies, Art Deco etchings, postwar cartoons, and contemporary commercials. Rabbits are also found as decorative elements of ceramics, buttons, fabrics, and collectibles.

Rabbits have been well represented throughout the history of literature, from the writings of Aristotle to *Alice's Adventures in Wonderland.* In folklore, they represent both craftiness and folly, bravery and cowardice. And they are particularly prevalent in children's books. In almost all of these cases, the literary representations of rabbits inspired artistic representations as well. Beatrix Potter's charming illustrations for *The Tale of Peter Rabbit* are as revered as the stories themselves.

Joseph Beuys. *Friedenshase.* 1982. Gold, pearls, and precious stones in steel safe with thick glass, 13¼ x 13¼ x 8⅛". Staatsgalerie Stuttgart

799th Bombardment Squad
469th Bombardment Group
AAB Alexandria, La.

World War II insignia depicting Walt Disney's character Thumper. © The Walt Disney Company

Disney's animated rabbit, Thumper, joined the war effort as a troop insignia. Rabbits played an even more significant role in U.S. war plans as gas detectors. Caged rabbits were kept near mustard and nerve-gas storage facilities. If a leak occurred, rabbits quickly showed symptoms of gas poisoning, allowing the army to evacuate soldiers and civilians.

References to this creature abound in contemporary art and culture. Artists as diverse as Joseph Beuys and Jennifer Bartlett have included rabbits in their work. Bugs Bunny and Thumper are twentieth-century pop icons who share the spotlight with advertising's Energizer Bunny.

Rabbits really are found everywhere, not only in art, literature, mythology, and popular culture, but also in geography (Coney Island), sports (the rabbit punch), dance (the bunny hop), and even botany (hare-parsley, harebell). Some speculate that both plant names derive from

Up n'Atom. Vegetable box made
for Watsonville Company. c. 1950s.
Private Collection

HARES

Above:
Logo for Hares Antiques, Cirencester, England. Courtesy Jennifer Hare, Cirencester

Lepus europaeus. Postage stamp. Designed by R. Iliev, Bulgaria. Issued 1993, 1⅛ x 1½"

Boy with Whip. Made by Althof, or Bergmann (?). c. 1874. Tin, height 3½". Collection Bernhard Barenholtz

The toy at right was photographed in front of The Rabbit, a well-known business-luncheon club in Philadelphia.

Opposite:
Postage stamp. Designed by Celestine Piatti, Duggingen, Switzerland. First-day cover, issued November 26, 1990, ¹⁵⁄₁₆ x 1⅛"

HELVETIA 70

C. PIATTI   1991   M. MÜLLER

myths, although it is more likely that the harebell was so named because it grew near rabbit warrens, and hare-parsley is a favorite food source of rabbits.

In presenting only a sampling of rabbit imagery, the following pages nevertheless will reveal a wide assortment of rabbits from around the world. As a constant companion to human beings throughout the ages, the rabbit has represented almost every human aspiration, ranging from the fear of life to the desire for eternal life, from sexual profligacy to sexual purity. In other words, representations of the rabbit are as varied and contradictory as human nature.

Milos Forman, Warren, Connecticut, 1993. Photograph by Mary Ellen Mark

Playmates. Designed by M. I. Hummel. 1930s. Painted porcelain, height 4″. Courtesy W. Goebel Porzellanfabrik, Rödental, Germany

In 1919, when this photograph was taken, its prizewinning subject, Prince Stanhope, an eight-month-old rabbit weighing sixteen pounds, was valued at $150,000. His owner apparently was not sentimental about rabbits, however; she is wearing a stole made from the fur of Prince Stanhope's father, Prince Leo, a former Grand Champion among American rabbits.

فقال أرنب منهن يقال له فيروز وكان معروفا بالدها والأدب
والحيل لا يخاف ان النبله ابعث معي رسولا يسمع قولي وينظر الى مقالتي
فقال ملك الأرنب انت وثوق عندنا وأنا نريد عليك شاهدا
لأنك لست بالمتهم عندنا فاذهب بالرأي وأطاع وانظر الذي ترى
فأتني الأبه واعلم الفيله به   واعلم أن الرسول هو الذي بسط الأمر لو

"What's Up, Doc?": Rabbits as Symbols

A Saxon Idol of the Moon. Illustration from *A Restitution of Deceived Intelligence,* by R. Verstege. Antwerp, 1605

Opposite:
Fairuz, the Hare, Addressing the Hares. From the manuscript of Bidpai, *Kalila wa Dimna.* Probably Syria, 1354. MS Pococke 400, folio 98r. The Bodleian Library, Oxford

Right:
Takuma Shoga. *Moon Goddess.* Japan, 1191. Section of a folding screen, painted silk

The screen depicts twelve *devas*, or gods and goddesses. The moon goddess holds a crescent moon in which a white hare is seated.

An ancient Saxon illustration, *Idol of the Moon,* depicts a goddess wearing a rabbit chapron over her head and shoulders. The moon-disk she holds in front of her abdomen represents pregnancy. This version of the hare-goddess is no longer worshiped in Europe, but a mythological rabbit is still prominent in the celebration of Easter.

A connection between the rabbit and the moon can be seen in the mythologies of almost all of the world's civilizations. Rabbits are featured in the astrological and zodiacal signs of many civilizations as well. In many myths, the rabbit, the moon, and fertility are all tied together. One legend from the Far East holds that the female hare becomes impregnated by running across the surface of the water under a full moon; however, if the moon is obstructed by clouds or mist, the hare will not conceive. In another version of the story, female hares become pregnant just by staring at the full moon. And, in a third version, the female hare conceives by licking the fur of the male when the moon is full.

In the West, many speak of "the man in the moon"; however, the Japanese speak of "the hare in the moon." In Japan, the rabbit is believed to keep the moon clean, which it does by rubbing it with a bunch of horse-tails. The word for moon in Sanskrit is *cacadharas,* which translates as "one who carries the hare."

As a common target of hunters, the rabbit was associated with Artemis in ancient Greece. Many Greek terra-cotta figurines depict women holding rabbits. Several are representations of Artemis with her bow, a lion, and a rabbit. Artemis was described as loving the hunting of rabbits, although she protected their young. Xenophon noted that, during the hunt, newborn rabbits were not killed but were left to Artemis.

The founding of the Greek city of Boiai in Laconia is attributed to a mythological rabbit. The citizens prayed to Artemis and Aphrodite to show them where to live. When a rabbit appeared before them, they followed it until it disappeared under a myrtle bush. On that site they built their city.

The hare sleeps with its eyes open, which added to its magical reputation. The animal often symbolizes an "opening." Although the hare was known to have poor eyesight, it was also believed to be constantly vigilant; watching over everyone, even at night, like the moon. This was true not only in ancient Egypt but in Rome as well. Camerarius used the rabbit to represent *Vigilandum,* the need for watchfulness.

According to Buddhist legend, Buddha appeared as a hare during one of his earthly incarnations. He was approached by a starving beggar who asked for food. Buddha told the man to make a fire and then he threw himself into it, sacrificing himself so that the man could eat. The beggar turned out to be the god Indra, who rewarded the "rabbit's" noble gesture by imprinting his image upon the face of the moon.

The red hare, another divinity in China, often appears with the phoenix and the unicorn as harbingers of peace and prosperity. The black hare was believed to come from the North Pole with greetings from the moon goddess. The appearance of a black hare portended a successful reign.

Rabbits (or coneys) and hares are mentioned only twice in the Bible. In Leviticus 11:4–6, Moses prohibits them from being eaten. In Deuteronomy 14:7, he reiterates the message:

> Nevertheless these ye shall not eat of them that chew the cud, or of them that divide the cloven hoof; as the camel and the hare, and the coney; for they chew the cud but divide not the hoof; therefore they are unclean unto you.

Rabbits were also considered taboo as food by residents of the British Isles under Roman rule. Julius Caesar even noted that the Britons "may not eat the hare, chicken, or the goose, but keep these animals for pleasure." The hare was proscribed food in ancient Africa by the Abyssinians and the Galla as well.

The rabbit is a favorite folkloric hero in Africa. In the tales of the Bushmen, the rabbit was once a man who took on his present shape after being cursed by the moon for his stupidity. This transformation from human to animal form also appears in the African-derived Uncle Remus stories.

Wall painting. Egypt, c. 2040–1080 B.C. From
the tomb of Inkerka, Deir El Medina,
Thebes, Egypt. Musée du Louvre, Paris

The painted scene shows a hare challenging
the serpent, Apep, an incarnation of
the sun-god, who appears to be guarding
a sacred tree.

Right:
Ba Birds and Shadow. Egypt, 1307–1196
B.C. Mural from the tomb of Irynefer,
Thebes, Egypt

In Egyptian pictographic writing, the
hare signified the consonant combination
wn, which was used in forming the word
meaning "to be." Rabbit hieroglyphs
figure prominently in the background
writing on this mural. See bottom right
and above the top bird's right wing, for
example.

Above:
Vase painting depicting the moon goddess giving birth to a rabbit, at right. At left, Goddess O (the midwife) presents the rabbit for nursing. Mexico, Maya culture, A.D. 600–900. Painted and fired ceramic, height 6 ¾", diameter 4". Museum of Fine Arts, Boston

Below:
Vase painting depicting rabbits as phases of the moon, leading to an eclipse. Mexico, Maya culture, A.D. 600–900. Painted and fired ceramic, height 5 ⅞", diameter 4". Private Collection

Below:
Ritual calendar symbols. From the Codex Laud, Misc 678, page 9.
Mexico, Mixtec culture, 1200–1521. The Bodleian Library, Oxford

The rabbit was one of four different year signs in this ancient
Mixtec calendar. A series of accompanying graphic details next to
the rabbit head establish the precise year of each entry.

Ceramic whistle in the form
of the moon goddess, Ix-chel,
and her consort the rabbit-in-
the-moon. Mexico, Maya
culture, Late Classic period,
A.D. 600–800. Clay with
traces of red and Maya
blue pigment, 4⁵⁄₁₆ x 3″.
The Art Museum, Princeton
University. Lent anonymously

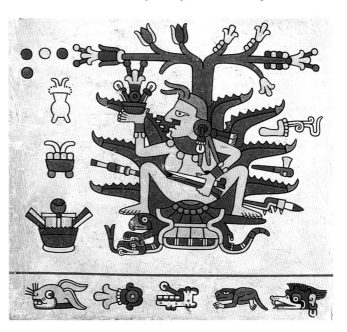

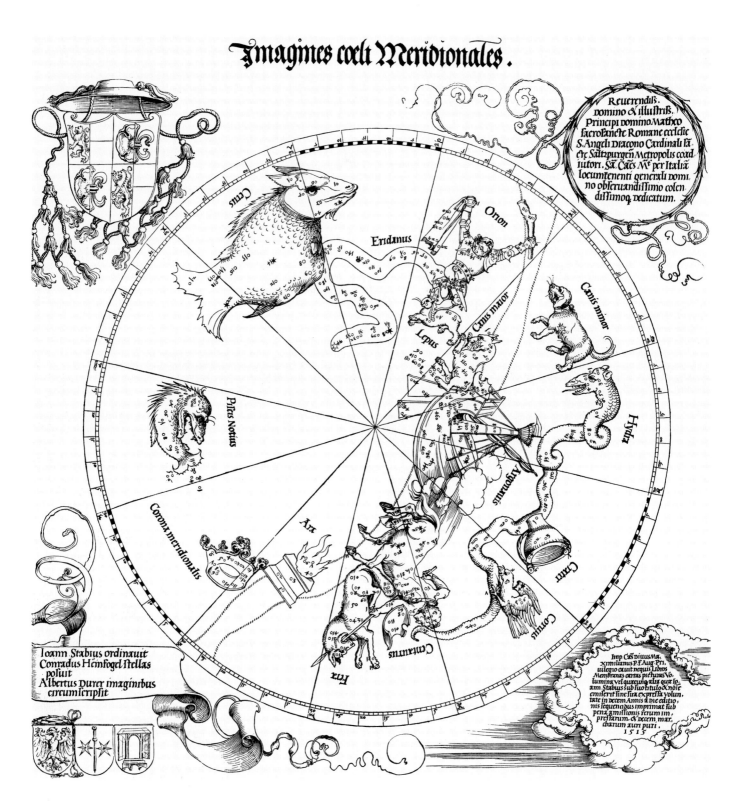

Imagines coeli Meridionales.

Reuerendiss.
domino & illustriss.
Principi domino Matheo
sacrosancte Romane ecclesie
S. Angeli Diacono Cardinali sa
cre Saltzpurgen Metropolis coad
iutori. Sa. Caes. Ma. per Italiam
locumtenenti generali domi.
no observandissimo colen
dissimoq, dedicatum.

Ioann Stabius ordinauit
Conradus Heinfogel Stellas
posuit
Albertus Durer imaginibus
circumscripsit.

Imp Caes diuus Ma.
ximilianus P.F. Aug. Pri,
uilegio cauit nequis Libros
Membranas certas picturas Vo
lumina vel quecumq, alia que Io.
am Stabius sub suo titulo & noie
emiserit sine sua expressa volun.
tate in decem Annis a die editio.
nis sequentibus imprimat sub
pena amissionis rerum im.
pressarum. & decem. mar.
charum auri puri.
1515

Albrecht Dürer. *The Southern Celestial
Hemisphere.* 1515. Woodcut, 17¹³⁄₁₆ x
17⅛". Rosenwald Collection, © 1994
Board of Trustees, National Gallery
of Art, Washington, D.C.
1954.12.234 (B-21422) / PR

Opposite:
Umar al-Sufi. *Lepus as Seen in the Sky.*
From a copy of Abd al-Rahman's *Book
of Fixed Stars (Suwar al-Kawakib al-
Thabitah).* Islamic, 1009–10 A.D. MS
Marsh 144, page 342. The Bodleian
Library, Oxford

كوكبة الأرنب على ما يرى في الكرة   كوكبة الأرنب على ما يرى في السماء

عرش الجوزا

جدول كوكبة الأرنب بزياداتي ... مثبت على ما في المستقيم

أسما الكواكب

	أسماء الكواكب	الطول		العرض		العظم
ا	الشمالي من الضلع المتقدم ذي الاربعة الاضلاع الذي على الاذن	كب	ب	له	لط	د
ب	الجنوبي من الضلع المتقدم	ب	د	لب	لو	د
ح	الشمالي من الضلع التالي	ب	د	له	له	د
د	الجنوبي من الضلع التالي	ا	د	لو	لو	د
ه	الذي في الذقن	ا	يد	لط	لط	د
و	الذي على اليد اليسرى من المتقدم	كج	يح	مه	به	د
ز	الذي في وسط البدن	ل	ح	لب	ما	د
ح	الذي تحت البطن	ل	د	كد	مد	ه
ط	اميل الاسرى للبدن و الرجل الموخرة الى الشمال	صب	د	بد	مه	د
ل	اميلهما في الجنوب	د	ند	نه	د
ا	الذي على العطن	مه	كد	لح	كد	د
س	الذي على طرف الذنب	كب	ع	لح	لع	د

فلك يب كوكبا منها في العظم الثالث ب وفي الرابع ح وفي الخامس د

Lepus americanus. Reverse side of Canadian coin, 5 cents. 1967. Nickel, approximate diameter ⅘". Collection Gerhard Schön, Munich

Lepus timidus. Reverse side of Irish coin, 3 pence. 1928–68. Nickel (cupronickel since 1942), approximate diameter ⅔". Collection Gerhard Schön, Munich

Pronolagus crassicaudatus. Reverse side of Tanzanian coin, 50 senti. 1966–90. Cupronickel (nickel-plated steel since 1988), approximate diameter ⅘". Collection Gerhard Schön, Munich

Opposite:
Hare rosette from Paderborn Cathedral. Germany, early 16th century. Carved stone. Courtesy, Erzbischöfliches Diözesanmuseum, Paderborn

The inscription for the rosette reads, "Each hare has two ears; together they have only three."

Figure of a rabbit "giving birth." Mexico, Aztec culture, 1350–1521. Jadeite, height 7⅛". Dumbarton Oaks Research Library and Collections, Washington, D.C.

The seated rabbit wears a broad belt adorned with skulls and crossbones, attached to the front of which is a warrior's head in an eagle helmet. The eyes were once inlaid.

Opposite:
Francesco del Cossa. Detail of *Month of April*. 1469–70. Fresco from the Room of the Months, Palazzo Schifanoia, Ferrara, Italy

Right:
Antonio Pisanello. *Allegory of Luxury*. 1430. Pen and bister on paper, prepared with red chalk, 50¾ x 59⅞". Graphische Sammlung Albertina, Vienna

Among its many symbolic representations, the rabbit has stood for sensuality, luxury, and an overactive libido.

Playboy, a men's magazine with strong sexual content, is represented by the silhouette of a now world-famous bunny, a modern example of the time-honored link between rabbits and sex. The phrase "mad as a March hare" further reinforces the rabbit's connection to sexuality. Traced back to an aphorism of Erasmus, this expression refers to the spectacular zeal with which rabbits unite during mating season.

Aristotle remarked on the connection between these animals and sex. And in a bas-relief of *The Lay of Aristotle*, on the facade of the cathedral of Saint-Jean in Lyons, the rabbit stands for the sexual temptation that humiliated the philosopher.

Until the end of the eighteenth century, it was widely believed that the rabbit could change its sex. In *Have with You to Saffron Walden*, Thomas Nashe wrote, "Shall we have a hare of him then a male one yeare and a female another?"

In ancient Rome, the rabbit was depicted as the animal of Venus, the goddess of love, and rabbit meat was often prescribed as medicine for sexual deficiencies. Classical works described the realm of Venus (Aphro-

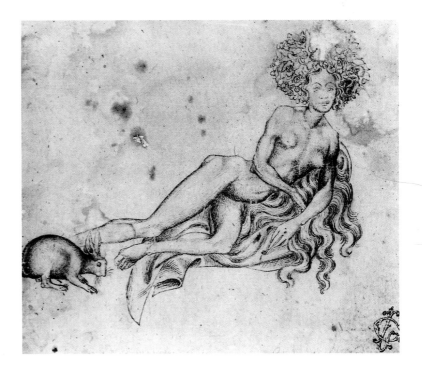

dite to the Greeks) as a place where cherubs chase rabbits. The Greeks often depicted rabbits in the company of Aphrodite and Cupids and in the Dionysian rituals, as seen on an amphora from 540 B.C. of Dionysus with Maenads.

According to Philostratus, hares were the most appropriate sacrifice to the goddess Aphrodite: "You know of course the legend of the hare, that it possesses the gift of Aphrodite to a superlative degree." The "gift of Aphrodite" was fertility, which the person making the sacrifice hoped to receive. Philostratus also recounts a story of a woman who miscarried seven times but finally gave birth after her husband unexpectedly presented her with a rabbit.

The rabbit was a fertility symbol in the mythology of various North American Indian tribes as well. During the "rabbit dance," male and female participants circled a drum while imitating the mannerisms of a rabbit. The purpose of this ritual was to increase fertility in the tribe and also to please the rabbits so that they would make themselves easier to hunt.

Due to the high rate of infant mortality during the Middle Ages, the ability to have many children was revered. Rabbits are often the first animals to give birth in the spring, and they are able to procreate many times a year. Medieval and Renaissance artists frequently included them in their tapestries as a tribute to their enviable fertility.

To the Greeks, rabbits were a traditional "love-gage." They were presented as totems of love from one person to another. Many classical scenes represent men offering rabbits to women; sometimes the women are shown just after receiving this gift of love. In many examples, rabbits are being offered to men by other men. In these cases, the rabbits have the same connotation.

Rabbits have equally symbolized chastity and purity. During the Middle Ages and the Renaissance, rabbits—white rabbits in particular—were often included in depictions of the Madonna and Child; here, the timid, defenseless creatures represent unquestioning faith in Christ. In Titian's *Madonna with the Rabbit*, the white rabbit being held by the Madonna also stands for the control over and purification of sexuality.

Another reason for rabbits' presence in images of the Madonna and Child is that, throughout the Middle Ages, people believed the female rabbit could conceive without a male. Some medieval encyclopedists even thought the rabbit could give birth without ever losing its virginity, further strengthening the rabbit's association with Mary and the "Virgin Birth."

This duality of sexuality and fertility, purity and chastity is common among many rabbit symbolisms. As Shakespeare wrote in *The Taming of the Shrew*:

I knew a wench married in an afternoon as she went to the garden
for parsley to stuff a rabbit; and so may you, sir: and so, adieu, sir.

Titian. *Madonna and Child with Saint Catherine*
(called *Madonna with the Rabbit*). 1530.
Oil on canvas, 27¾ x 33". Musée du Louvre, Paris

i am the handmaid of the earth · i broider fair her glorious gown.
and deck her on her days of mirth · with many a garland of renown.

and while earth's little ones are fain · and play about the mother's hem
i scatter every gift i gain · from sun and wind to gladden them.

35

Page 34:
Giovannino de' Grassi. Initial letter of the *Magnificat*. From the *Book of Hours of Gian Galeazzo Visconti*. c. 1385. National Library, Florence

Page 35:
The Flora Tapestry. Designed by Edward Burne-Jones (figure) and William Morris (background). Woven 1885 at Merton Abbey. Wool and silk on linen warp, 9'10½" x 6'10½". The Whitworth Art Gallery, University of Manchester, England

William Morris was inspired by the tapestries of the Middle Ages and the Renaissance, in which rabbits often represented fertility. Their influence can be seen in his textile designs.

Rabbit Head Logo. Courtesy of Playboy Enterprises

Joseph Cornell. *Untitled (Robert Cornell modification, rabbit head)*. 1968. Collaged reproductions, Masonite, glass, cellophane tape, masking tape, wood; 16¹⁄₁₆ x 12¹⁄₁₆ x ⅞". Collection Walker Art Center, Minneapolis. Gift of The Joseph and Robert Cornell Memorial Foundation, 1993 [93.233]

Opposite:
Woman with Rabbit Hat. Cover of *Theatre Magazine*, April 1924. Signed Baskerville. Private Collection

As a symbol of fertility, the rabbit has always been strongly associated with women. This image from 1924 is reminiscent of the later Playboy Bunny. It also echoes the ancient Saxon Idol of the Moon, who wore a similar rabbit chapron over her head and shoulders.

APRIL
24

THEATRE
MAGAZINE

35
cents

BASKERVILLE

Happy Easter

This gay Easter bunny
is bringing good cheer
And greetings galore
through the mail.
He hopes that your joys
are as long as his ear
And your worries
as short as his tail.

EASTER
GREETINGS

A Joyful
EASTERTIDE

EASTER
GREETINGS

A JOYOUS EASTER!

I am sending you this
Easter greeting
from a heart filled with
good wishes.

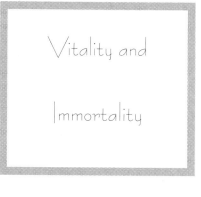

K. F. Edmund von Freyhold. *Easter Bunny.* 1920s. Illustration

Opposite:
Easter postcards. Turn of the century. Private Collection

Prolific breeders, rabbits are natural symbols of rebirth—an important element in the Easter tradition. Even in ancient times, before Easter was celebrated, rabbits were popular icons of springtime.

Right:
Handkerchief. Late 19th–early 20th century. Cotton. Courtesy of the Design Library, New York

Everyone loves the spring season. It is a time of rebirth and renewal; flowers bloom, leaves reappear, and love blossoms. One of the most evocative symbols of springtime is the rabbit. In ancient Greece and Rome, spring rituals prominently featured rabbits. Perhaps the most famous spring rabbit of all is the Easter Bunny.

Rabbits' astonishing ability to reproduce and the fact that they are often the first animals to give birth in the spring make them popular symbols of rebirth and encourage the natural pairing of the rabbit with the Easter holiday. Also, since the Council of Trent in A.D. 325, Easter has been celebrated on the first Sunday after the first full moon of spring, in keeping with the traditional association of the rabbit and the moon.

In Germany, the Easter Bunny is called *Osterhase.* An old folktale from Bavaria describes a poor mother who had no money to buy Easter presents for her children. Instead, she decided to paint some eggs, which she then hid in the woods. Later, according to the tale, her children were

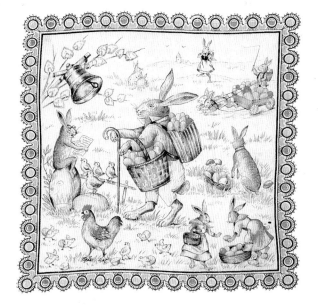

playing and spotted a rabbit. They followed the bunny into the woods, and it led them to the hidden basket of painted eggs. Naturally they believed the rabbit had left them the eggs as an Easter present, and the legend has grown from there.

Katsu Jagyoku. *Rabbits and Pine Trees in the Snow.* Japan, Edo period, 1774.
Ink and white pigments on paper, 5′ 9/16″ x 11′ 6 15/16″. Etsuko and Joe Price Collection

In Far Eastern mythology, rabbits were believed to create the elixir of life that bestowed eternal youth upon the drinker.

In England, people tried to catch rabbits in an Easter contest. One folk tradition held that whoever brought a rabbit to church on Easter Sunday before ten o'clock in the morning would receive one hundred eggs for breakfast.

In art and literature, rabbits are often symbols of immortality. The Chinese depicted them with a mortar and pestle, pounding out the elixir of life. In fact, the Chinese believed that the hare itself was created from the covering of "the pill of immortality."

The Chinese also believed that rabbits live to be incredibly old. When they reach one hundred years of age, their fur turns white, and when they reach five hundred years, their fur turns blue. Throughout the East, rabbit meat was thought to be a cure for various diseases and an important source of vitality.

On Greek and Roman tombs, rabbits are portrayed eating figs or grapes, images representing rebirth. This age-old connection between rabbits and rebirth and vitality is still present in our popular culture. The corporate logo for The Nature Company is a rabbit, in part symbolizing the eternal essence of the natural world.

The Algonquin Indians believed that the rabbit god, Manabozho (Big Rabbit), was the incarnation of all life-giving energy. And it is no coincidence that Energizer Batteries features a rabbit in its extremely successful marketing campaign. Just like Manabozho, the Energizer Bunny "just keeps going, and going, and going..."

Wall painting from Herculaneum, showing a rabbit eating figs. c. 1st century B.C.–1st century A.D. National Archaeological Museum, Naples

A popular subject in ancient Rome, rabbits appear in mosaics and paintings and on ceramics and carved border details in Rome, Ravenna, Gurgi, and Herculaneum.

Don Nice. *Jack-Rabbit.* 1976.
Watercolor, 75 x 40″. Collection of
Julia and Carter Walker, New York.
Courtesy Nancy Hoffmann Gallery,
New York

ازین حدیث عجب آمد بسوی چشمه رفت صورة ماه در آب دید به روزا و را گفت ای ملک

قدری فطوم بردار و ویرا سجده دیگای آرش دید که ماه در مقام ترحم آمده از تو راضی کرده دیل فطوم درآن کرد

آسیب خرطوم مثل آب رسید و کت در آب رسید و پل بدید آمد و پل را جنبانید کرد که ما به هم جنبیدآ و از داد که ای کس

ماه که بدانجه جرم خرطوم در آب کردم از جای بیشد دلی روز گفت آری زود تر سجده کن تا قرار گیرد دل فطوم

برداری نمی و قبول کرد که پیش ازین آنجا نیایده و پلا نا از انجا الی آن چشمه نیارد به روز خبر بیشه برد خبر کوشش

ایشه مذدار جمله بلا جنان ازین منبع دفع کرد ید

44

Speed and Cunning

Yip, my name's Molly cotton-tail,
Catch me if you can.
—*THE TALE OF THE RABBIT AND THE TAR BABY*

Opposite:
The Elephants and Hares at the Well, Called Fountain of the Moon. From an *Anwar-i-Suhayli* manuscript, copied and illustrated at Ahmadabad, India, with Mughal miniatures. 1600–1601. Gouache on paper, 6½ x 5⅛". MS OR 6317, folio 114r. By permission of the British Library

"He who, owing to a successful effort against a weak enemy, is led to believe that his strength is irresistible, often pays dearly for his presumption, in a contest with a more powerful opponent, and you, O king, relying on your superiority over the other beasts, overlook the consequences of your temerity in drinking at and polluting the Fountain of the Moon, who has directed me to caution you against a repetition of this insult, threatening, in case of your disobedience, not only to withdraw the light which she so graciously dispenses, but to effect your destruction; and if you have any doubts about my mission, I will accompany you to the Fountain, and convince you of the truth of it."
—the "Ambassador" of the Moon
to the king of the elephants,
from Jessica Rawson, *Animals in Art*

Right:
The Hare and the King of the Elephants at the Well of the Moon. From the manuscript of Bidpai, *Kalila wa Dimna.* Probably Syria, 1354. MS Pococke 400, folio 99r. The Bodleian Library, Oxford

The "Tar Baby" tales traveled to America with African slaves. While many regional variations of the stories exist, all end with the rabbit escaping his doom by using his speed and cunning. The classic version recorded by Joel Chandler Harris in the Uncle Remus stories has the tar-covered Br'er Rabbit using reverse psychology to fool Br'er Fox into throwing him into the briar patch. Once there, Br'er Rabbit scampers away safely.

The rabbit appears frequently in the role of the clever trickster in many cultures, including throughout Africa and in the mythologies of many tribes of American Indians. The Algonquins' Manabozho was infamous for his trickery, and many of their folktales record his exploits. The trickster rabbit is also a fixture in Eastern folklore. In the often-illustrated story of "The Fountain of the Moon," clever hares devised a ruse to stop

the elephants from trampling them when they came to drink at the communal watering place. One of the hares disguised himself as the Ambassador of the Moon and warned the king of the elephants about the dangers of engaging a more powerful enemy. The next time the elephant drank at the fountain, the hare convinced him that the quivering reflection of the moon meant that the mighty moon was mad at the elephants for trampling the hares. Thus fooled, the elephants promised to change their ways. This and other fables were a source of imagery in many miniature paintings of the famed Mughal court artists.

In real life, rabbits are capable of great cunning. When hunted, they often elude their pursuers by running in circles. They are also known to hide in bushes, jump into bodies of water, and sneak into hollow trees to escape.

The artistic representation of the clever rabbit continues today. One of the most popular cartoon characters ever created is Warner Bros.' Bugs Bunny. Bugs is a classic trickster rabbit, smart, cruel, and resourceful. Bugs Bunny rarely beats his opponents with physical force; instead, he outwits them, using his craftiness and quickness.

Speed is a defining characteristic of all rabbits and an important element in the adventures of Bugs Bunny. Always able to appear and disappear far quicker than those who hunt him, Bugs can also change outfits in a fraction of a second and slip out of Elmer Fudd's rifle sights in the blink of an eye. His speed and smarts enable him to torture Yosemite Sam without ever being harmed himself.

Bugs Bunny is not the only rabbit to embody speed. Volkswagen created a successful line of automobiles, called Rabbits, whose logo is an image of a rabbit running at top speed.

The speed and cleverness of the rabbit are less positive factors in the Aesop's fable of "The Tortoise and the Hare," in which the hare possesses great physical speed but is cocky and overconfident, common attrib-

Ceramic tile illustrating the story of "The Tortoise and the Hare," from *Aesop's Fables.* Designed by John Moyr Smith for Mintons China Works. c. 1875

utes of the trickster rabbit. In the end, the hare is embarrassed by the slow, plodding tortoise. While Bugs Bunny almost always succeeds, the traditional trickster rabbit often loses the contest he starts.

Arthur Burdett Frost. *Br'er Rabbit.*
c. 1890. Watercolor and pencil, 14⅜ x 10¾".
Sterling and Francine Clark Art Institute,
Williamstown, Massachusetts

Bugs Bunny. ™ and © 1995 Warner Bros.

Perhaps the most famous rabbit in popular culture
today is Bugs Bunny, who first became famous
as a cartoon character and has crossed over into
advertising, fashion, and collectibles.

Jerry Pinkney. *Br'er Rabbit and the Tar Baby.* Illustration from *The Tales of Uncle Remus,* retold by Julius Lester. New York, Dial Books, 1987

The Br'er Rabbit tales originated with the folklore of Africa. Brought to this country by African slaves, Br'er Rabbit is a classic example of the tradition of the "trickster rabbit."

למה חרו לך
ולמה נפלו פניך · למה
ליחיים · וכשיהיה על האהע
יהיה מלי יערפי למה אמרת
למה העליתנו למה עזבתני
למה היברת העביר · ובאו
בדגש ובלייע על האא ועל ההא
למה אבכה לתה איא במירע
למהיה כאב נגה למה הרגתנו
למה הציתו עבדיך · ובא רפי ובלרע
זולתי על אות גרועת למה שכתב
למה נחרב · ובא רפי ומליע למה
תבבי ולמה לא תאכלי ולמה ירעלבך
אבל עם הבת הוא ברגש ומלרע יכבה
ידע איפה · ובבה יתריה זה האדע

מן ובתוספת יוד והנו בצרי מעדיך
מן ארח · ובחירק הנון מע אפרס
דנשות הנן בשה מפני הטפות המלה
כי לא יתבן מבל דרגש אסלא ילדרנה
בונהם · ובכנו ישבשנו ממיס ממנו
ממע ובמס אחת לברה שעמני לעשו
עצה ולא מע · ובמנולהם גברו מנג ·
ממך · וברהפסק מך ובמס אחת לברה
מהם מכב והמדברים בעדם ממנו והמם
בדנש כמו לנסתר להסרוןנונמן והעענ
מבדיל בין מרביים בערם

כי ידברו עליהם
בכלל ופרט · וכן על היחיד
פעמים · ואי פשרגם כן כי גם
המה לשון רבים ואפ שאמר
משכיל פירושו על כל משל
ומשובל · וכן ויטר יצלימו בלחמו
על כל רשע וערשע · ובמותם
כתבנו ורבים בתחל זה הספר
אבל ישר יחז פנמו הוא כני היחיד
או הוא ודרך כבד כמו אור עשי
והדומיסלו מה מימתי
אין בהם קבוץ
וכנו · ומה בלמין ובדחיק בפתה כמו
מהברי מה בינע מה פרעת זהו בסנו
בבד מקומות על פי המסורת · ויל האחית
ועל הי נע ליעלם בסנול זולתי ז מקומות
ה קמ מה עבדי כי מה עבד הכלב
ואמרת על מה על בני יי · ויאמר ליה
מה יצבדת · ומה חשך · וב פתחי מה
חטאתי כי מה רפינו · וכן הוא פתח
ליעלם עשהוא ועשהיא · ונכנמו הבית
והכף על מה בפת עשה הרבשולא להסרון
הא הדייה · במה אדע כמה מי ישב
חייך · ובא בשוא במה שיהיה אחריו
וכשתכנס עליו הלמר גם כן ברנש אא
שהוא מליעל והוא כלו קמין

Fear and Cowardice

The Greek historian Polybios gave rabbits the name *Kyniklos*, meaning, "animals that live in an underground system of burrows." Their habit of hiding out underground, coupled with a natural tendency to flee, help explain why rabbits have long been associated with timidity and cowardice.

Aristotle and Chaucer also made reference to the rabbit's inherent timidity. In the Middle Ages, the word "rabbit" was used to describe a timid soldier. Even today, the term "rabbit ears" is used to describe someone who is afraid. Many artistic depictions of rabbits are based on their helplessness. Often the timid creatures were used as symbols for humankind's need to put the hope for salvation and trust in God.

Opposite:
An Army of Hares Besieging a Wolf in His Castle. Arcaded page of David Kimhi's grammar compendium, *Sefer Mikhlol.* Corunna, Spain, 1476. MS Kennicott, folio 442v. The Bodleian Library, Oxford

As cute as many people find them, rabbits have also inspired fear. They have been interpreted as bad omens for centuries. In medieval Hungary, the appearance of a rabbit was believed to presage a fatal accident. In England, they were seen as omens of impending fires.

Right:
The Unclean Spirit. From *The Cloisters Apocalypse*, folio 333v. c.1320. Color, gold, silver, and brown ink on vellum, 12⅛ x 9". The Metropolitan Museum of Art, New York. The Cloisters Collection, 1968.68.174

In this medieval manuscript illumination, Christ confronts a dragon, a beast, and a false prophet from whose mouths spew froglike evil spirits. Off to one side, a rabbit cowers in his burrow.

Leonardo da Vinci noted these qualities in his bestiary, where he mentioned that rabbits are often frightened by falling leaves. Lewis Carroll's White Rabbit from *Alice's Adventures in Wonderland* is constantly in a rush because he is afraid of the Queen of Hearts. Mark Twain also noticed that rabbits were easily frightened. In his short story "In the Animals Court," Twain describes a rabbit who is tried, convicted, and hanged for cowardice and desertion. As Twain points out, the rabbit had no choice but to follow the "law of God, which denies courage to the rabbit."

Paradoxically, at the same time the rabbit has been a symbol of fearfulness it has also been a creature that evokes fear in others. In part, rabbits have inspired fear because they were associated with mischief and misfortune. Rabbits were thought to be bewitched animals and, as such, often were seen as incarnations of witches. The Celts believed that rabbits spent so much time underground because they were in contact with the netherworld. In Fifeshire, fishermen would tremble at the sight of a rabbit, even a dead one.

Master Nicolas of Modena. Animal frieze. 12th century. Carved stone. Cathedral apse, Königslutter, Germany

Johan Schaper. Cup depicting hares executing hunters. c. 1665, Germany. Free-blown enameled glass; height 2⁹⁄₁₆", diameter 2⁹⁄₁₆". Gift of Edward Drummond Libbey, The Toledo Museum of Art, Ohio. 1950.37

Page 54:
Viking Ship and Creeping Things. Second quarter 11th century. MS Regin. Lat. 12, folio 108r. Biblioteca Apostolica Vaticana, Rome

During the Middle Ages, rabbits were often looked on with dread. Here they are included in a list of fearful, "creeping things," along with sea monsters and tropical beasts.

rspatiosummanib:

nonest numerus·

magnis·

ibunt·

sti adilludenduei·

tdesillis escāintēpore·

apiente tē manum

ntur bonitate·

ciem turbabuntur·

& deficient·

ruestentur·

creabuntur·

terrę·

ilum·

rib: suis·

acit eam tremere·

fumigant·

The Vikings grouped the rabbit with sea monsters and tropical beasts among their depictions of fearful creatures. In Islamic poetry, a monster called Al-mi'raj is described as a yellow hare with a single black horn on its head.

A rabbit monster leaps out of a magician's hat in *Twilight Zone, The Movie.* In the film comedy *Monty Python and the Holy Grail,* King Arthur and his men are attacked by a tiny but vicious rabbit, prompting the king to utter the military order, "Run away!"

While amusing, the rabbit scene from *Monty Python and the Holy Grail* is also based in historical fact. Two demonic hares sculpted in the medieval Collegiate Church in Königslutter dance over a bound, prostrate body. They seem to represent pure evil. And sculpted into the south porch of the Cathedral of Chartres is an image of a soldier dropping his sword and fleeing in terror from an approaching rabbit. Also sculpted into the south portal of Chartres is a monstrous rabbit carrying off a woman.

During this period, coming into contact with a rabbit was thought to be unlucky, yet at the same time it was considered good luck to carry a rabbit's foot. Actually, carrying any part of a rabbit (tail, ear, or innards) was said to bring good fortune, but the foot was believed to be the most powerful totem. Originally, people hoped that by carrying the rabbit's foot some of the animal's fertility might rub off on them.

THE HARE

In the black furrow of a field
I saw an old witch-hare this night;
And she cocked a lissome ear,
And she eyed the moon so bright,
And she nibbled of the green;
And I whispered "Whsst! witch-hare,"
Away like a ghostie o'er the field
She fled, and left the moonlight there.

—Walter de la Mare

Detail of *The Last Judgment.* 1194–1220. Carved stone. South portal, Chartres Cathedral

The two-part scene shows a demon in the form of a rabbit approaching a young woman. In the second carving, the woman has been flung over the demon's shoulder, her hair trailing behind.

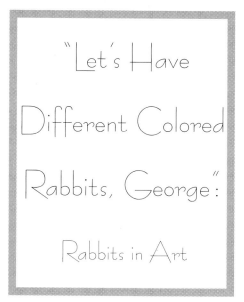
Lepus, Kyniklos, Lagos, Sason, the terms for "rabbit" survive from even the most ancient civilizations. The rabbit has been portrayed in art ever since the earliest images were recorded. The Egyptians used a rabbit hieroglyph meaning "to be." The Nile valley was full of rabbits, and in most Egyptian tomb representations they are included among food offerings to the dead. Depicted in the ancient Egyptian temple of Dendera are two hare-headed gods. One is male and the other is a goddess known as Unnut, who is also mentioned in the seventeenth chapter of the Egyptian Book of the Dead. In ancient Assyria, palace carvings featured hares as trophies from the hunt or as supplies for a banquet.

During the Ice Age, huge numbers of rabbits migrated to what is now Spain. The first written report of these animals comes from the

Opposite:
Angiolo Leone. *San Domenico and San Francesco.* c. 1620. Oil on canvas, 84⅝ x 39⅜". Sacristy, St. Giovanni, Venice

Right:
A Peasant Holding Two Hares. Egypt, c. 1400 B.C. Tomb painting, 13 x 9". Copyright British Museum

Phoenicians, who observed them off the Spanish coast. They called the land *i-shaphan-im.* The word *shaphan* (meaning "sly" or "crafty") referred to the Phoenician rock hyrax, which bore a great resemblance to the Spanish rabbit. Therefore, the Phoenicians' name for Spain was in English, "coast of the island of rock hyraxes." The name was later translated by the Romans into *Hispania,* which in English became Spain. On some Roman coins, a rabbit sits between the goddess Minerva and an olive tree symbolizing Spain. The Roman writer Catullus' phrase describing Spain, *cuniculosa Celtiberia,* is often translated as "rabbity Spain." Strabo wrote that the inhabitants of the

Coin. Messina, Sicily, c. 425 B.C. Silver coin, diameter 1". Copyright British Museum

Depicted on the face of the coin is a running or leaping hare. The cicada below is an engraver's symbol.

Balearic islands sent an emissary to Rome to request a new homeland. Apparently, the proliferation of troublesome, burrowing rabbits made the islands almost uninhabitable.

Many Greek urns and amphorae feature rabbits. A Panathenaic amphora from about 490 B.C. depicts a victorious athlete receiving a tribute that includes a dead hare. In ancient Rome, rabbits were kept on the game reserves of the wealthy. Eagles would often attack and carry the rabbits off in their claws, a scene featured on many Greek and Roman coins. In the Greek version, the eagles stand for the Greek armies and the hare represents vanquished Troy. This metaphor comes from a passage in Aeschylus's *Agamemnon,* where two eagles attacking a pregnant hare is interpreted as an omen presaging victory over the Trojans for Agamemnon and Menelaus.

The rabbit was a common artistic subject among various civilizations in India, China, and Japan. Rabbits are depicted in a series of Chinese amulets from the Zhou period (fourth century B.C.), which were often found in graves. A popular subject in China among painters of the Song period, rabbits are also represented in the chase scenes from the Qin tomb tiles as well as in some Han bronzes and stone bas-reliefs. In a Japanese painting on silk by Takuma Shoga from A.D. 1191, the moon goddess, Gwatten, holds a moon in her hands. Inside the moon is a white rabbit. In Japan, the hare was often depicted as the companion of Kintoki (the bear). The rabbit is also featured in Japanese literature. Two popular folk tales, *The White Hare of Inaba* and *Kachikachi Yama (The Crackling Mountain),* include important rabbit characters, each described as clever tricksters.

The rabbit and the moon are often associated throughout Far Eastern art (see also page 21). Frequently the rabbit is shown pounding

Tetradrachmon coin with eagle and rabbit. Greece, c. 413–411 B.C. Silver coin, dim. n.a. Private Collection, London

Eagles with Serpent and Hares in
Talons. Byzantium (Constantinople).
11th century. Marble relief.
Copyright British Museum

Above and left (detail):
Amasis Painter. Dionysus with
Maenads. c. 540 B.C. Black-figure
decoration on a ceramic amphora,
height of amphora 13″.
Bibliothèque Nationale, Paris

Tapestry fragment. Coptic, 6th century.
Wool, 7⅛ x 7⅞". Musée Historique des
Tissus, Lyon

Mounted Huntsman Attacking a Hare.
3rd–4th century A.D. Mosaic. Piazza
Armerina, Sicily

The Creation of the Animals, detail of *The Dome of the Creation.* c. 12th–13th century. Mosaic. Narthex, San Marco, Venice

Noah Freeing the Animals from the Ark.
c. 12th–13th century. Detail of ceiling
mosaic. Atrium, San Marco, Venice

Hans Witschi. *Studio 6*. 1984. Oil on canvas, 34 ⅝ x 41". Private Collection

rice flour or making rice cakes known as *mochi,* which means both "rice cakes" and "full moon" in Japanese. Rabbits played an important role in some of the ancient civilizations from what is now Mexico. In the Mixtec calendar, the rabbit was one of the four "year-bearer" signs. Rabbit heads establishing the date can be seen throughout the decorative motifs in manuscripts, calendars, and screenfolds of this period (see also pages 24–25).

Today, rabbits appear in movies, cartoons, calendars, posters, periodicals, and as logos for businesses as well. Animated rabbits have enjoyed great success as clever tricksters (Bugs Bunny), faithful friends (Thumper), and fools (Roger Rabbit). Rabbits have been featured on the cover of *Harper's* Magazine, in the shadows of the feature film *Harvey,* and even starred in their own horror movie, *Night of the Lepus.*

Publicity still. From the Universal Pictures Company feature film *Harvey*, 1950

The rabbit is often portrayed as a faithful best friend. In the movie version of *Harvey*, Jimmy Stewart's inseparable pal is an invisible six-foot-three-inch rabbit.

I'm Having the Weirdest Sense of Déjà Vu. From *The Big Book of Hell*, © 1989 by Matt Groening. All Rights Reserved

Before creating the Simpson family, Matt Groening developed a series of comics titled *Life in Hell*, featuring some very unique rabbits.

Choju Giga (Frolicking Animals).
Handscroll (fragment). Japan,
Kamakura period, 13th century.
Ink on paper, 11⅜ x 21⅛".
Kosan-ji, Toganoo, Kyoto

In the *Choju Giga,* animals enact
human roles in scenes that both
mock and pay homage to Buddhist
rituals.

Barry Flanagan. *Hare on Bell on Portland-Stone Piers.* 1983. Bronze, limestone, 8′6″ x 9′4″ x 6′3″ overall. Collection Walker Art Center, Minneapolis. Gift of Anne Larsen Simonson and Marilyn and Glen Nelson, 1987 [87.63]

Pastoral Rabbits

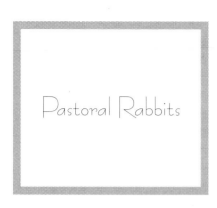

Giovannino de' Grassi. *Goat, Hare, Wolf, and Leopard*. From the *Taccuino di Disegni*. 1395. MS, folio 16. Biblioteca Civica, Bergamo

Opposite:
Albrecht Dürer. *Hare*. 1502. Watercolor and body color on very mildew-flecked paper, brush, heightened with white, traces of preliminary drawing on the right ear, 9⅞ x 8⅞". Graphische Sammlung Albertina, Vienna

Right:
Antonio Pisanello. *Study of a Hare*. From the Vallardi Codex (no. 2445). Second quarter 15th century. Pen, black chalk, and watercolor on paper, 5 ½ x 8 ⅞". Musée du Louvre, Paris

Rabbits have long been a favorite subject in still lifes, nature studies, and landscapes. The sixteenth-century German artist Albrecht Dürer was responsible for dozens of drawings and watercolors of rabbits. Dürer's series of rabbit images has been referred to as the first example of a self-contained nature study. In these figures, he strove to express both the physicality and the personality of his subject. In several drawings, engravings, and woodcuts, he included rabbits cavorting with Cupids. After Dürer's, the most well-known rabbit studies were executed by Hans Hoffmann and Joris Hoefnagel.

Dürer's interest in rabbits may have been formed by viewing some of the paintings of two of his favorite Italian artists of an earlier generation, Andrea Mantegna and Giovanni Bellini, who both incorporated rabbits frequently in their work. Many artists in the Italian Renaissance included rabbits to lighten the mood of otherwise somber pieces. Some portraits from this period depict women holding rabbits, which were often kept as pets.

The rabbit also makes an appearance in manuscript illuminations from both the East and the West. In a fourteenth-century Syrian manuscript, *Kalila wa Dimna*, the rabbit Fairuz addresses a group of fellow rabbits. And in the *Taymouth Horae*, a British manuscript from the same century, a monk is depicted on a hare hunt. Medieval monks often hunted and bred rabbits as an important food source.

69

Left and above (detail):
Albrecht Dürer. *The Glorification of the Virgin.* c. 1504.
Woodcut, 11⅝ x 8⅜" (full image). Rosenwald
Collection, © Board of Trustees, National Gallery of
Art, Washington, D.C. 1943.3.3592 (B-6617)/ PR

Rabbits were a popular element in many
Renaissance artworks, where they were
depicted as companions to Apollo, playmates
for the infant Jesus, and diversions for
suffering saints.

Opposite:
Hans Hoffmann (after Dürer). *Hare Seen from
Above.* 1528. Watercolor and gouache, 14 x 10¼".
Staatliche Museen zu Berlin, Preussischer
Kulturbesitz: Kupferstichkabinett

Cy deuise du lieure et de toute
sa nature.

Ieure est asses
conuuie beste
si ne me cou
uient ia dire
de sa facon.
car pou de gens
sont qui bien nen ayent veu.
il viuent des blez et autres gaig
nages de herbes de fueilles de escor
ces darbres de raisins et dauaius
autres fruiz. moult est bonne
bestelete vn lieure et moult y a

de plaisance en la chasce plus q̃
en beste du monde par. v. raisõs
si ne treust si petite chose. Iune
car tout lan sa chasce dure sen;
riens esparguier. et de nulle
autre beste ne le fair. Et aussi
le peut on chascer au uespre
au matin. au uespre quant
sont releuees. au matin quãt
sont alees au giste. et des autres
bestes non. car sil pluet au ma
tin vous autre; pour vne iournee
et des lieures non. Lautre le q̃
ur et cerchier vn lieure est trop

TVTE LEPVS ES ET PVLPAMENTVM QVAERIS

LEPVS DORMIT.

Joris Hoefnagel. *Hares, Raurackl, and Squirrel. From Animalia Quadrupedia et Reptilia (Terra)*, plate 47 c. 1575–80. Watercolor and gouache, pen, brush, heightened with white, encircled with oval border in gold, on vellum, 5⅝ x 7¼". Gift of Mrs. Lessing J. Rodenwald, © 1994 Board of Trustees, National Gallery of Art, Washington, D.C. 1987.20.6.48/ DR

Raurackl was the name given to a mythical horned rabbit, or "stag-hare." In Bavaria it was known as a *Woltpertinger*. Originating in the tall tales of hunters, the raurackl was brought to life by various artists, including Hoefnagel.

Albrecht Dürer. *Rabbits*, details from *The Triumphal Arch of Maximilian*. 1515 (1799 edition). Forty-two woodcuts and two etchings on laid paper assembled to form one image, 11'2³⁄₁₆" x 9'7¹⁄₁₆" overall. Gift of David P. Tunick and Elizabeth S. Tunick in honor of the 50th Anniversary of the National Gallery of Art, © 1994 Board of Trustees, National Gallery of Art, Washington, D.C. 1991.200.1/PR

Opposite:
Rabbits in a Meadow. From the *Hunting Book of Gaston Phébus.* c. 1450. MS 1291, folio 5. Bibliothèque Nationale, Paris

Lelio Barsovrcnon
Lura 1587

74

Opposite:
Attributed to Hans Hoffmann. *Hare.*
1587. Watercolor and body color on
paper, 5¹¹⁄₁₆ x 4⅜″. Staatliche Museen zu
Berlin, Preussischer Kulturbesitz:
Kupferstichkabinett

Above:
Hans Hoffmann. *Hare beneath a Tree.*
c. 1550–91. Point of brush and
gouache, heightened with white, on
vellum laid down on panel, 10¹¹⁄₁₆ x 7″.
Collection of Diane Woodner and
Andrea Woodner, New York

The rabbit has long been a favorite prey of hunters, perhaps in part due to a common belief described by Pliny the Elder:

> The common sort of people are persuaded, that the meat of this kind of venison (i.e., Hare's flesh) causeth them that feed upon it to look fair, lovely and gracious, for a week together afterwards. There must needs be some cause and reason of this settled opinion, which hath thus generally carried the world away to think so.

Whether or not eating rabbit meat really does improve one's appearance, its popularity as prey is evidenced by the many images of the rabbit as hunting trophies, from the walls of Egyptian tombs to the still lifes of the Renaissance to American frontier paintings of the nineteenth century.

Hunting Scene, with Three Hounds Driving Two Hares into a Net. First half 12th century. Fresco from San Baudeliode Berlanga, Soria, Spain. Private Collection

Many methods have been used to hunt rabbits. The Greeks used nets and clubs. A Greek bronze statue of Pan shows him carrying a *lagobolon*, a special club thrown at hares *(lagos)* while hunting them. The Phoenicians used ferrets to force rabbits out of their burrows and into nets.

The proliferation of rabbits on the Iberian peninsula led to the wide-scale introduction of ferrets into that country. The Romans used this method as well, although they preferred dachshunds to ferrets. An early twelfth-century fresco at San Baudelio de Berlanga in the Spanish province of Soria depicts three hounds driving two rabbits into a net.

Many nature studies of rabbits focus on anatomy rather than symbolism. Their significance as symbols, however, is never far behind. During her period of captivity, Mary, Queen of Scots frequently embroidered an image of some hares walking over a lion trapped in a net. Written beneath this pastoral image was the Latin phrase, *Et lepores devicto insultant leone* (Even hares trample on the conquered lion).

Opposite:
Hare Hunt. From the *Taymouth Horae.* c. 1350. Yates Thompson MS 13, folio 69v. By permission of the British Library

The monks of the Middle Ages hunted and bred rabbits as an important food source. They also continued the Roman tradition of eating unborn and infant rabbits. Rabbits were not considered to be meat, so the monks could even eat them during fasts.

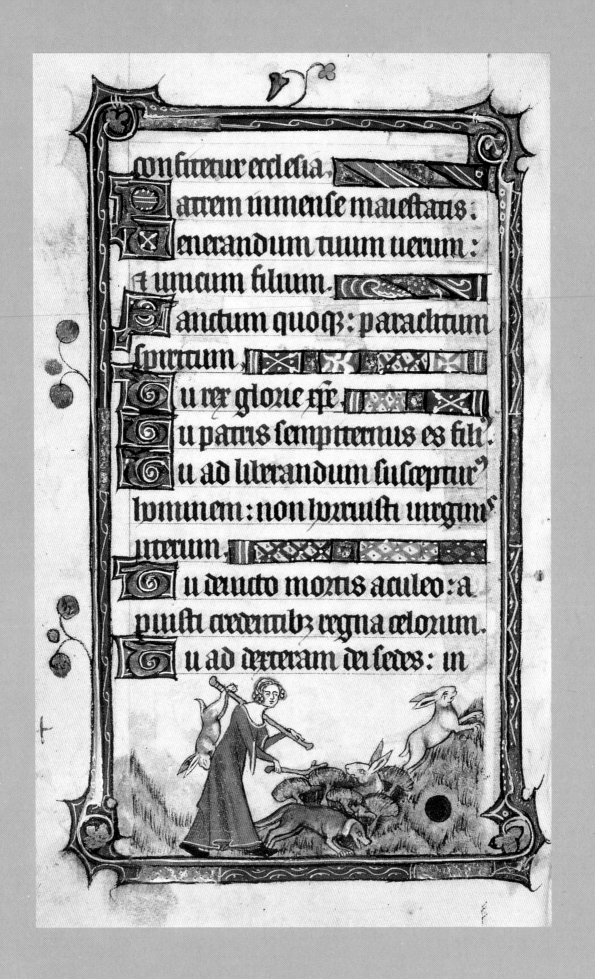

confitetur ecclesia.

atrem immense maieftatis:

enerandum tuum uerum:

t unicum filium.

anctum quoqȝ: paraclitum

spiritum.

u rer glorie rpe

u patris sempiternus es fili.

u ad librandum susceptur

hominem: non horruisti uirginis

uterum.

u deuicto mortis aculeo: a

puisti credentibȝ regna celorum.

u ad dexteram dei sedes: in

Jean-Baptiste Siméon Chardin. *Rabbit,
Copper Cauldron, Quince, and Chestnuts.*
c. 1726–28. Oil on canvas, 26¾ x 22⅜".
Nationalmuseum, Stockholm

W. M. Harnett. *After the Hunt,* fourth version. 1885. Oil on canvas, 70½ x 47½". Mildred Anna Williams Collection, The Fine Arts Museums of San Francisco

W. R. Rodgers wrote, "A farmer of my acquaintance in County Armagh assured me that the hare really enjoys being hunted. As proof of this he adduced the case of a hare which had reared her young close up against the back of a hounds' kennel on his farm. 'It liked,' he said, 'to be near the hounds.'"

Hare among Buds and Flowers. Toledo, Spain, 16th century. Cuenca tile with worn relief, 3⅞ x 3⅞". Collection, Museum Boymans-van Beuningen, Rotterdam

Opposite:
Joan Miró. *Still Life with Rabbit (The Table)*. 1920–21. Oil on canvas, 51⅛ x 43". Collection Gustav Zumsteg, Zurich

Perhaps due to the great number of rabbits in Spain, that animal is featured in many Spanish artworks, such as the tile above and still life by Joan Miró opposite.

Folding screen. Japan, Kano School, c. 15th–18th century

For both religious and mythological reasons, rabbits have had great
significance throughout the Far East; however, in many Japanese images,
the rabbit is just a rabbit—a study in nature rather than a symbol.

Opposite:
Satoshi Yabuuchi. *Rabbits in a
Forest.* 1992. Bronze, height
15¾", length 14⅜" (each rabbit).
Private Collection

Literary Rabbits

The earliest literary examples of rabbits come from ancient folk tales, where they are traditionally described as cunning tricksters. There are many such examples from India, including the tale in which a rabbit escapes death by fooling a lion into fighting his own reflection.

Rabbits were often mentioned in the literature of ancient Greece and Rome, by Xenophon, Philippus of Thessalonica, Meleager, and others. In Homer's *The Iliad*, the wounded Hector compares himself to a dead lion insulted by hares.

The rabbit features in the writings of the Middle Ages as well. In *The Canterbury Tales*, Geoffrey Chaucer describes the Monk's love of hunting:

Grehoundes he hadde as swift as fowel in flight;
Of prikyng and of huntyng for the hare
Was al his lust, for no cost wolde he spare.

The Monk enjoyed chasing after rabbits, but Chaucer was making a pun with the word *hare*, which also stands for "whore" or women in general.

Rabbits appear frequently in the work of William Shakespeare. They are mentioned in *Venus and Adonis*, *As You Like It*, *Twelfth Night*, *Troilus and Cressida*, *Coriolanus*, and *Romeo and Juliet*. In *King Henry IV, Part I*, Shakespeare coined the term *hare-brained* to describe Hotspur's audacity. And in *King Henry IV, Part II*, he used the rabbit as an insult: "Away, you whoreson upright rabbit, away!" Many other poets included rabbits in their work. Robert Burns described the rabbit's gait as *hirpling*, John Keats evoked a hare trembling in the frozen grass, Wallace Stevens penned, "A Rabbit as King of the Ghosts," and William Wordsworth wrote of a frolicking hare on a warm spring morning:

The hare is running races in her mirth;
And with her feet she from the plashy earth
Raises a mist; that, glittering in the sun,
Runs with her all the way, wherever she doth run.

Illustrations of rabbits often accompanied their literary references. They were frequently included in illuminations of medieval bestiaries and

Howard Penfield. Cover of *Harper's* Magazine, Easter issue, March 1895

scenes of the Creation. Often they were used as elements in political cartoons. In Walter Crane's book *The First of May, A Fairy Masque*, he included pencil drawings of playful rabbits. And approximately one hundred years later, the hidden treasure hinted at in Kit Williams's *Masquerade* was a jeweled rabbit.

Among the most beloved of literary rabbits is Br'er Rabbit, who was always getting himself into and out of trouble. One of the most famous

THE POINT.

In the original caption to this caricature, Joseph Chamberlain, Britain's Secretary of State for the Colonies, as Br'er Fox, asks Boer leader Kruger, as Br'er Rabbit, how he would like to be cooked:

"Br'er Rabbit up en say he don' wanter be cooked t'all.

"Br'er Fox he grit his toof. 'Youer gittin' 'way from de point, Br'er Rabbit,' sez Br'er Fox, sezee.'"

rabbits in Western literature is the White Rabbit from *Alice's Adventures in Wonderland*. He is the only character (aside from Alice) who passes between the real world and Wonderland. When he orders Alice to fetch his gloves and fan, Alice says to herself, "How queer it seems to be going messages for a rabbit!" Even though he is a fictional character, the White Rabbit is aware of real rabbit concerns:

> It was the White Rabbit, trotting slowly back again,
> and looking anxiously about as it went, as if it had
> lost something; and she heard it muttering to itself,
> "The Duchess! The Duchess! Oh my dear paws! Oh my
> fur and whiskers! She'll get me executed, as sure as
> ferrets are ferrets!"

A snappy dresser who is constantly in a rush, the White Rabbit was first illustrated by Sir John Tenniel in the book published in 1865. More recently, rabbits have appeared in Robert Adams's *Watership Down*, John Steinbeck's *Of Mice and Men* and *The Grapes of Wrath*, and John Updike's series of works chronicling the life of a man named Harry (Rabbit) Angstrom.

Opposite, above:
Sir John Tenniel. *White Rabbit.* Engraving. Reproduced in *Alice's Adventures in Wonderland,* by Lewis Carroll. London, Macmillan, 1865

Opposite, below:
Sir John Tenniel. *March Hare.* Engraving. Reproduced in *Alice's Adventures in Wonderland,* by Lewis Carroll. London, Macmillan, 1865

Arthur Rackham. *A Mad Tea-Party.* Illustration from *Alice's Adventures in Wonderland,* by Lewis Carroll. London, William Heinemann, 1907

Opposite:
Arthur Rackham. *Why, Mary Ann,*
What Are You Doing Out There?
Illustration from *Alice's Adventures in*
Wonderland, by Lewis Carroll.
London, Wm. Heinemann, 1907

Mike Twohy. Cartoon.
From *Animals, Animals,*
Animals, copyright © 1979
by The Cartoonists Guild,
Inc. All Rights Reserved

Decorative Rabbits

Rabbits have been represented as decorative elements throughout the history of ceramics, textiles, and fabrics. They can be seen in Coptic tunics from the sixth century A.D. and in Easter fabrics more than thirteen hundred years later. Persian ceramic plates from the early fourteenth century depict rabbits. They decorate Italian majolica platters from the fifteenth century and Spanish floor tiles from the sixteenth century. These creatures even appear on soup tureens, Hummel figurines, cookie jars, and salt and pepper shakers.

Rabbits are incorporated into jewelry too. Some pieces fuse images of them from antiquity with modern settings. In the Middle Ages, couples often exchanged rabbit rings during the wedding ceremony in hopes of increasing their fertility. During the Italian Renaissance, necklaces were adorned with ornamental rabbits. And they were so adored as pets during this period that, when they died, tombs and funerary odes were created to help console their grieving mistresses. More recently, Cartier made a rabbit-shaped bell push with precious stones, enamel, gold, and silver.

Especially popular in Japan, rabbits are the subject of everything from paintings to lacquer boxes and buttons. Rabbits have also been represented on countless pins, postcards, stamps, and even on paper money.

Opposite:
Pair of rabbits. 1987. Boxwood ojime, length ⅞"; signed Wraight. Miriam and Robert O. Kinsey Collection

The rabbit is the fourth of twelve zodiac animals, which designate a twelve-branch cycle of years derived from the Chinese lunar calendar. The concept was popularized in the myths of Japan as well as those of China, India, and Korea. People born in the year of the rabbit often wore a rabbit ojime as a symbol of the attributes of virtue, skill, and intelligence associated with their birth year. The rabbit ojime also symbolizes the beauty of moonlight.

One-ruble bill

Buttons. Japan, late 19th–early 20th century. Etched ivory, average length 1″.
Collection of Diana Epstein and Millicent Safro, Tender Buttons, New York

Rabbit between Tall Grass. Probably 2nd half 19th century. Black lacquer box with gold and silver decoration and red lacquer [eyes], ojime of cast metal with geometric design; box 2⅝ x 1¾"; signed Chôshûsai Bunri or Fumishige. Linden-Museum, Stuttgart

These writing cases were invented in China, but they received much more attention in Japan. The Japanese versions, called *suzuribako*, were made of metal, ceramic, and lacquered wood and were often lavishly detailed.

Rabbit pendant. Flanders, c. 1590. Enameled gold,
four pearls, 1⅝ x 1″. Silver Museum, Florence

Rabbits were beloved pets during the Renaissance.
Sometimes when they died, their distraught
mistresses commissioned funerary odes to them.

Brooches. Designed by Elizabeth Gage. 1993. Clockwise from top:
bronze rabbit (Roman, 3rd century A.D.), farm token (16th century)
surrounded by 18k gold and red enamel clubs, South Sea pearl;
bronze rabbit (Roman, 3rd century A.D.), carved green tourmaline
surrounded by repoussé gold with blue enamel; bronze rabbit
(Roman, 3rd century A.D.), carved fire opal surrounded by 18k
planished gold with black enamel. Diameter of largest brooch
approximately 1¾". Courtesy Elizabeth Gage, London

Above:
Rabbits. Designed by Daniel Swarovski. 1988. Crystal, (from left to right) 1⅛ x 1⅜″, 1¼ x 1⅛″, 2⅛ x 1⁹⁄₁₆″. Courtesy Daniel Swarovski Corporation, Feldmeilen, Switzerland

Below:
Medicine bottle. Germany, 16th century. Green glass and wire, 6⅞ x 5¹¹⁄₁₆″. Germanisches Nationalmuseum, Nuremberg

Rabbit. House of Cartier, Paris. c. 1904.
Amethyst with ruby eyes and diamond collar,
1¾ x ¾ x 1⅝″. The Cartier Collection

Opposite:
Bell push. House of Cartier, Paris.
c. 1906. Agate rabbit with sapphire eyes;
base of turquoise and white enamel on
silver, encircled by a wavy motif of gold
leaves; base diameter 3½", height 1⅜".
Lindemann Collection

Above:
Snuffbox with two rabbits on a mound.
Mennecy, France, mid-18th century. Painted
porcelain, hinged silver mount, height 1⅜",
length 2". Victoria & Albert Museum, London

Two rabbits. The Netherlands, 1600–1650.
Frieze tile, 2⁷⁄₁₆ x 5⁵⁄₁₆". Collection, Museum
Boymans-van Beuningen, Rotterdam

Humpen glass. Germany (Bohemia?), late 16th century. Slightly gray-tinted glass with enameled cylindrical body, applied foot-ring; below rim: gilded band with rosettes and beads; height 10⁵⁄₁₆″. Copyright British Museum

The elaborate hunting scene spiraling around the sides of this vase includes a castle, hunters with dogs and nets, and their prey: rabbits, boar, stag, and bear.

Opposite:
Hunting goblet. Bohemia, 1597. Transparent deep-blue glass, blown, enameled, and gilded; height 10¹¹⁄₁₆″. Corning Museum of Glass, Corning, New York. Gift of Edwin Beinecke

Bowl. Iran? 9th–10th century (bowl), 10th–15th century (setting). Opaque turquoise glass, gold, gilded silver, precious stones; height 2⅜″, diameter 7⁵⁄₁₆″. Treasury, San Marco, Venice

Game-pie dish. Minton & Co. 1877. Majolica, length 18″. Courtesy Jeremy Cooper Ltd., London

Opposite:
Plate. Florentine, c.1450. Majolica, diameter 18½″. Victoria & Albert Museum, London

D'Arenberg Basin, made for Sultan Najm al-Din Ayyub. Egypt or Syria, c. 1240s. Brass, hammered and turned, chased and inlaid with silver and blank organic material, height 9⅛", diameter (rim) 19¹¹⁄₁₆"; inscription in Arabic. Courtesy of the Freer Art Gallery, Smithsonian Institution, Washington, D.C.

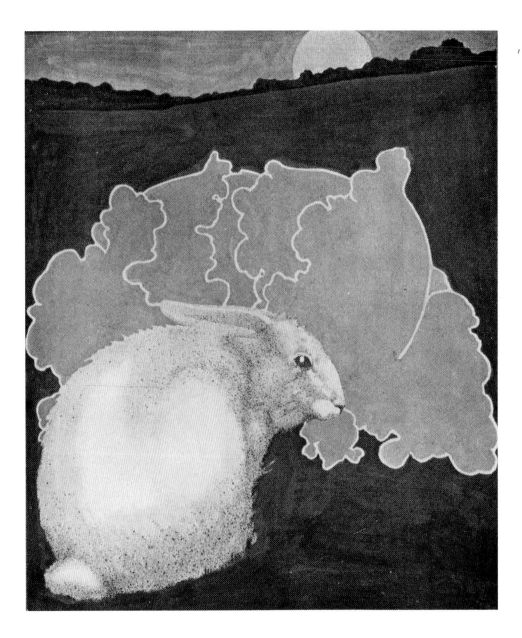

Above:
Maxfield Parrish.
Calendar illustration.
1906. Unidentified
calendar from a
Private Collection,
courtesy Mark
Gabor, New York

Gold Rab[b]it.
Matchbox cover.
Early 20th century.
Private Collection

Mr. and Mrs. Cottontail. Designed by Jan Kornfeind, sewn by Rosie Grinstead. 1989. Cotton quilt, machine-pieced, appliquéd and quilted by hand, 35 x 44½". Collection Rosie Grinstead, Mission Hills, Kansas

Bib clip. Webster Co., North Attleboro, Massachusetts. 1920s. Silver, length overall 7¼". Collection of Alexandra Venable, Dallas, Texas

Catering to parents wishing to instill table manners in their children, early twentieth-century silver manufacturers produced a variety of utilitarian objects in the shape of animals or incorporating scenes from fairy tales. These clips, placed around a child's neck, held a cloth napkin in place.

There was once a Velveteen Rabbit, and in the beginning he was splendid. He was fat and bunchy, he had real thread whiskers, and his ears were lined with pink sateen. On Christmas morning, when he sat wedged in the top of the Boy's stocking with a sprig of holly between his paws, the effect was charming.

—Margery Williams, *THE VELVETEEN RABBIT*

Rabbits are soft, docile, and cute, all of which make them ideal companions for children. Also, since rabbits produce offspring so frequently, the species as a whole is identified with youth and newness. Therefore, a lot of stories and artwork for children feature rabbits.

One of the most famous rabbits in children's stories and artwork is Beatrix Potter's Peter Rabbit. In 1893 Potter first crafted the story and the drawings in a series of letters sent to Noel Moore, the son of her former governess. The first letter began, "I don't know what to write to you, so I shall tell you a story about four little rabbits."

She later expanded these letters into *The Tale of Peter Rabbit*. When no one would publish it, she cashed in some bank stocks and did it herself in 1901; it was a moderate success. It was later republished by Frederick Warne and Company and sold extremely well. Peter Rabbit is now world famous, and Beatrix Potter went on to write several other successful books about rabbits, including *The Tale of Benjamin Bunny, The Tale of the Flopsy Bunnies*, and *The Story of a Fierce, Bad Rabbit*.

The rabbit frequently appears as a cherished companion to a youngster. Bambi's best friend was the rabbit Thumper. Winnie the Pooh often visited his pal Rabbit.

Stuffed toy rabbits are soft and cuddly and children love them. In *The Velveteen Rabbit*, a classic children's tale by Margery Williams, the hero is a stuffed rabbit who becomes real. Another popular book with very small children is Dorothy Kunhardt's *Pat the Bunny*, which even includes a swatch of imitation rabbit fur.

Children can find rabbits in toys, comic books, movies, cartoons, and even clothes. Magicians delight children, and adults, by pulling rabbits out of their hats, and sculpted carousel rabbits thrill both the young and the young at heart.

Benjamin Bunny, Flopsy, and the Flopsy Bunnies. Illustration from *The Tale of the Flopsy Bunnies*, by Beatrix Potter. London, Frederick Warne & Co., 1909

Opposite:
Peter Rabbit Eating Lettuces, French Beans, and Radishes. Illustration from *The Tale of Peter Rabbit*, by Beatrix Potter. London, Frederick Warne & Co., 1902

John Burnet, after David Wilkie. *The Rabbit on the Wall*. Engraving from
A Collection of Twenty-Nine Engravings after the Paintings of David Wilkie. London,
1811–15. Print Collection, Miriam and Ira D. Wallach Division of Art, Prints and
Photographs, The New York Public Library, Astor, Lenox and Tilden Foundations

This engraving represents the earliest known example of British shadowgraphy.

Ando Hiroshige.
*Sokkyo Kageboshi
Zukushi; Usagi to
Hachiue No Fukujuso
(Collection of Shadow
Games: Rabbit and
Potted Adonis Flowers).*
Japan, Edo period,
mid-1840s. Nishiki-e,
half oban, 14¾ x 10″.
James A. Michener
Collection, Honolulu
Academy of Arts

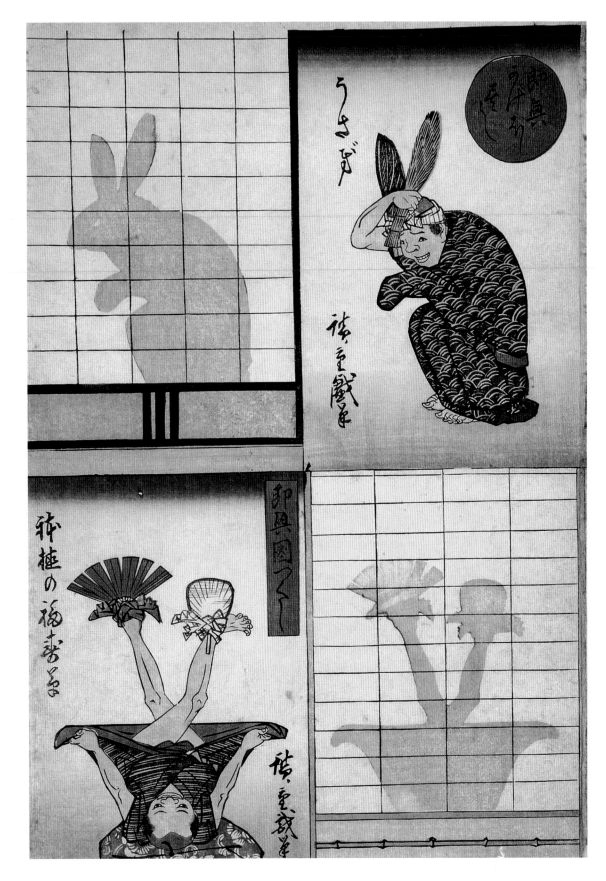

In 1953, Tony Curtis and Janet Leigh posed with a rabbit to promote their film biography of Harry Houdini.

Left:
World-famous magician Harry Blackstone pulling a rabbit out of a hat. 1943

Opposite:
Magician Performing a Hat Trick. 19th century. Woodcut

Young children love rabbits, and children of all ages love magic. It was only a matter of time before the two were paired.

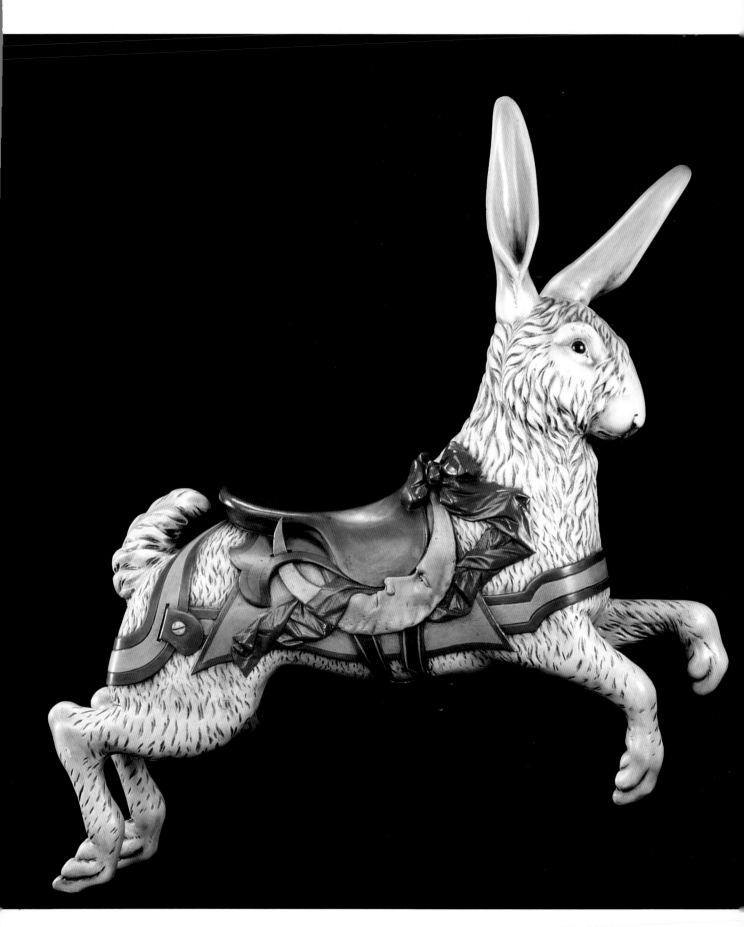

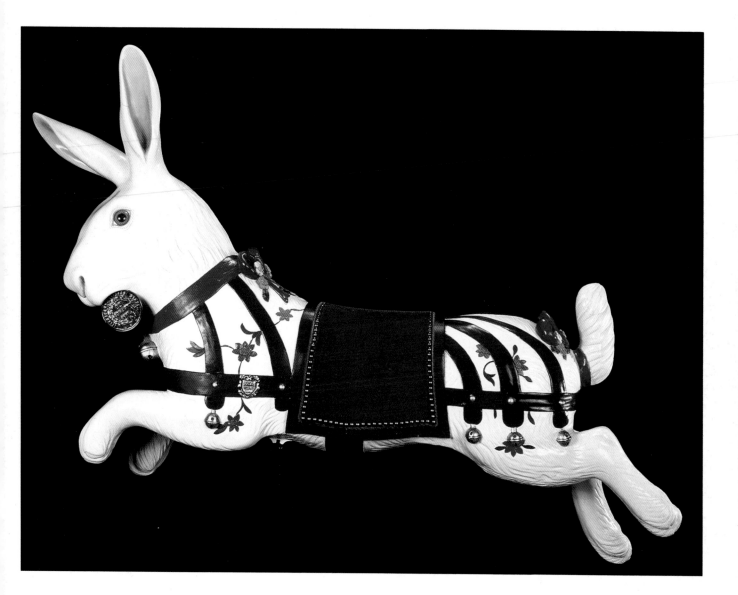

French carousel. c. 1899. Restored by Rol and Jo Summit.
Painted wood, 30 x 60″. Collection of Rol and Jo Summit

Opposite:
Dentzel carousel. c. 1908. Restored
by Maurice and Nina Fraley. Painted
wood, 60 x 50″. Collection of Mrs.
William H. Dentzel II and family

Rolling hoops. Made by Merriam. c. 1870s. Diameter of rabbit
hoop approximately 4½". Collection Bernhard Barenholtz

The rabbit hoop at left is considered among the rarest of its kind.
While many hoop toys feature children or dogs or other animals,
it is almost unheard of to come across a rabbit in a hoop.

Dog Chasing Rabbits. Pull toy. Made by Fallows. c. 1880s.
Tin, length 8¾". Collection Bernhard Barenholtz

Opposite:
Wind-up toy. Alps, 1950s.
Sheet metal, 3⁵⁄₁₆ x 2¹⁵⁄₁₆
x 8¼". Collection Teruhisa
Kitahara, Tokyo

Spring time

Summer days

Opposite:
William Nicholson. *Spring time.*
Illustration from *The Velveteen Rabbit*,
by Margery Williams. New York:
Doubleday and Co., 1958

Above:
William Nicholson. *Summer days.*
Illustration from *The Velveteen Rabbit*,
by Margery Williams. New York:
Doubleday and Co., 1958

Many popular children's books
prominently feature rabbits. In *The
Velveteen Rabbit*, the hero of the story
is a stuffed toy rabbit who dreams
of becoming a real bunny.

D. S. Moor. *Sovetskaya Repka (Soviet Turnip)*.
1920. Three-color lithograph, 28 x 17¾".
Uppsala University Library, BS 605

The scenes above are based on a popular
Russian children's story to which a political
moral has been added. The frog, the crow,
and the rabbit watch as Grandfather
Capitalism enlists the aid of his wife, child,
and various others in attempting to uproot
the Soviet turnip, who punishes them all
for their treachery.

Opposite:
And These Are Our Enemies.
Illustration from *Die
Hasenschule,* a children's
book. Leipzig, Germany,
Hahn Verlag, 1920s

Oswald the Lucky Rabbit. From the animated short
"The Old Swimming Hole." Used by permission from
The Walt Disney Company

Older even than Mickey Mouse, Oswald the Lucky
Rabbit was Disney's first successful cartoon character.
Oswald images and objects are still popular collector's
items today.

Roger Rabbit. From the Touchstone
Pictures & Amblin Entertainment
feature film *Who Framed Roger Rabbit?*,
1988. © The Walt Disney Company

Opposite, above right:
Publicity still. From the Warner Bros.
feature film *My Dream Is Yours*, 1949

In this film starring Doris Day and
Jack Carson, a young boy has a vivid
dream after being read a bedtime story
about Bugs Bunny.

Thumper and His Girlfriend. From the Walt Disney animated
feature film *Bambi*, 1942. © The Walt Disney Company

Easter Bunny. 1900s.
Illustration

Selected Bibliography

Animals in Ancient Art. Jerusalem: The Israel Museum, 1986. From the Middleburg Collection, Archaeological (Rockefeller) Museum.

Barclay, Joan. *African Animals in Renaissance Literature and Art*. Oxford: Clarendon Press, 1971.

Barenholtz, Bernard, and Inez McClintock. *American Antique Toys 1830–1900*. New York: Harry N. Abrams, Inc., 1980.

Beasts and Birds of the Middle Ages. Edited by Clarke, Willene B., and Meredith T. McMunn. Philadelphia: University of Pennsylvania Press, 1989.

Bevan, Elinor. *Representation of Animals in Sanctuaries of Artemis and Other Olympian Deities*. BAR International Series, 1986.

Brion, Marcel. *Animals in Art*. New York: Franklin Watts Inc., 1959.

Carroll, Lewis. *Alice's Adventures in Wonderland*. New York: Franklin Watts, Inc., 1907.

Carson, Gerald. *Men, Beasts, and Gods*. New York: Charles Scribner's Sons, 1972.

Clark, Kenneth McKenzie. *Animals and Men*. New York: William Morrow and Co., 1977.

Cotterel, Arthur. *The Macmillan Illustrated Encyclopedia of Myths and Legends*. New York: Macmillan Publishing Co., 1989.

Davies, Nina M. *Egyptian Tomb Paintings — From Originals Mainly of the Eighteenth Dynasty in the British Museum and the Bankes Collection*. London: Faber and Faber Limited.

Dembeck, Hermann. *Animals and Men*. New York: The Natural History Press, 1965.

Dent, Alan. *World of Shakespeare; Animals and Monsters*. New York: Taplinger Publishing Company, 1973.

Douglas, Norman. *Birds and Beasts of the Greek Anthology*. New York: Jonathan Cape and Harrison Smith, 1929.

Eisler, Colin. *Dürer's Animals*. Washington: The Smithsonian Institution Press, 1991.

Eliot, Alexander. *Universal Myths*. Meridian. 1976.

Evans, Edward Payson. *Animal Symbolism in Ecclesiastical Architecture*. New York: Henry Holt and Co., 1896.

Fraley, Tobin. *The Carousel Animal*. Berkeley: Zephyr Press, 1983.

Frankenstein, Alfred. *After the Hunt — William Harnett and Other American Still Life Painters — 1870–1900*. Berkeley: University of California Press, 1969.

Friedberg, Robert. *Coins of the British World*. New York: The Coin and Currency Institute, 1962.

Friedmann, Herbert. *A Bestiary for Saint Jerome: Animal Symbolism in European Religious Art*. Washington, D.C.: Smithsonian Institution Press, 1980.

Heide, Robert, and John Gilman. *Cartoon Collectibles — 50 Years of Dime-Store Memorabilia*. Garden City, N.Y.: Doubleday & Co., Inc., 1983.

Jenkins, G. K. *Ancient Greek Coins*. New York: Putnam's Sons, 1972.

Kitahara, Teruhisa. *Wind-Ups — Tin Toy Dreams*. San Francisco: Chronicle Books, 1985.

Klingender, Francis D. *Animals in Art and Thought to the End of the Middle Ages*. Cambridge: M.I.T. Press, 1971.

Kroeny, Fritz. *Albrecht Dürer and the Animal and Plant Studies of the Renaissance*. Munich: Prestal-Verlag, 1985, and New York: Little, Brown, and Co., 1988.

Laylard, John. *The Lady of the Hare*. London: Faber and Faber, 1944.

Lewinsohn, Richard. *Animals, Men and Mythology*. London: Victor Gollancz, 1954.

Lloyd, Joan Barclay. *African Animals in Renaissance Literature and Art*. Oxford: Clarendon Press, 1971.

MacDonald, Ruth K. *Beatrix Potter*. Boston: Twayne Publishers, 1986.

Mercatante, Anthony. *Zoo of the Gods*. New York: Harper and Row, 1974.

Milward, Peter. *An Encyclopedia of Flora and Fauna in English and American Literature*. Lampeter, Wales: The Edwin Mellen Press, 1992.

Phipson, Emma. *The Animal Lore of Shakespeare's Time*. London: Kegan Paul, Trench & Co., 1883.

Pinney, Roy. *The Animals in the Bible*. New York: Chilton Books.

Rabbits — A Classic Illustrated Treasury. San Francisco: Chronicle Books, 1993.

Rawson, Jessica. *Animals in Art*. London: British Museum Publications Ltd., 1977.

Rowland, Beryl. *Animals with Human Faces*. The University of Tennessee Press, 1973.

Schafer, Heinrich. *Principles of Egyptian Art*. Oxford: Clarendon Press, 1974.

Seager, H. W. *Natural History in Shakespeare's Time*. London: Elliot Stock, 1896.

Sowerby, Arthur de Carle. *Nature in Chinese Art*. New York: The John Day Company, 1940.

Stern, Harold P. *Birds, Beasts, Blossoms, and Bugs*. New York: Harry N. Abrams, Inc., 1976.

Toynbee, J. M. C. *Animals in Roman Life and Art*. Ithaca: Cornell University Press, 1973.

Van Buren, E. Douglas. *The Fauna of Ancient Mesopotamia as Presented in Art*. Rome: Pontificium Institutum Biblicum, 1939.

Wilkinson, Richard H. *Reading Egyptian Art*. London: Thames and Hudson, 1992.

Index

Note: Page numbers in *italics* refer to illustrations.

A

After the Hunt (Harnett), *79*
Alice's Adventures in Wonderland (Carroll), 52, *86, 87, 88*
Allegory of Luxury (Pisanello), *31*
Alps, toys, *116*
Amasis Painter, *Dionysus with Maenads, 59*
amphorae, *32, 59*
amulet, *13*
And These Are Our Enemies, 120
Animals in Council, The (Suhayli), *12*
Aphrodite, 22, 32
Aristotle, 31, 51
Army of Hares Besieging a Wolf in His Castle, An (Kimhi), *50*
Artemis, 21–22
Aztec figure, *31*

B

Ba Birds and Shadow (mural), *23*
Bartlett, Jennifer, *11 A.M., Bull Shirt, 10–11*
Baskerville, *Woman with Rabbit Hat, 37*
Bellini, Giovanni, 69
bell push, *98*
Beuys, Joseph, *Friedenshase, 14*
bib clip, *107*
Bidpai: *Fairuz, the Hare, Addressing the Hares, 20*; *Hare and the King of the Elephants at the Well of the Moon, 45*
Blackstone, Harry, *112*
Book of Fixed Stars (Rahman), *27*
bowl, *102*
Boy with Whip (toy), *16*
Br'er Rabbit (Frost), *47*
Br'er Rabbit and the Tar Baby (Pinkney), *48–49*
Bugs Bunny, 46, *47*, 64, 123
Burne-Jones, Edward, *Flora Tapestry, 35*
Burnet, John, *Rabbit on the Wall, 110*
buttons, *8–9, 92*

C

calendars, 25, *106*
Canterbury Tales, The (Chaucer), *85*
carousels, *114, 115*
Carroll, Lewis, *Alice's Adventures in Wonderland*, 52, *86, 87, 88*
Carson, Jack, *122, 123*
Cartier, House of, jewels, *97, 98*
cartoons, 46, *47*, 64, 65, 86, 89, 122
ceramic tile, *46*
ceramic whistle, *25*
Chardin, Jean-Baptiste Siméon, *Hare and Copper Cauldron, 78*

Chartres Cathedral, south portal, *55*
Chaucer, Geoffrey, 51; *Canterbury Tales, 85*
Choju Giga, handscroll, *66*
coins, *28, 58*
Cornell, Joseph, *Untitled, 36*
Cossa, Francesco del, *Month of April, 30*
Creation of the Animals, The, 62
crystal figures, *96*
cup (Schaper), *53*
currency, *91*
Curtis, Tony, *112*

D

D'Arenberg Basin, 104–5
Day, Doris, *122, 123*
de la Mare, Walter, *The Hare*, 55
Dionysus with Maenads (Amasis), *59*
Disney, Walt, *Oswald the Lucky Rabbit, 122*
Dog Chasing Rabbits (toy), *117*
Dürer, Albrecht, 69; *Glorification of the Virgin, 70*; *Hare, 68*; *Rabbits, 73*; *Southern Celestial Hemisphere, 26*; *Triumphal Arch of Maximilian, 73*

E

Eagles with Serpent and Hares in Talons, 59
Easter Bunny (Freyhold), *39*
Easter postcards, *38*
Easter rabbits, 21, *39*, 42, 84, *124*
Elephants and Hares at the Well, The, Called Fountain of the Moon (Suhayli), *44*
11 A.M., Bull Shirt (Bartlett), *10–11*

F

Fairuz, the Hare, Addressing the Hares (Bidpai), *20*
Fallows, pull toy, *117*
Flanagan, Barry, *Hare on Bell on Portland-Stone Piers, 67*
Flora Tapestry, The (Burne-Jones and Morris), *35*
Forman, Milos, *18*
"Fountain of the Moon," *44*, 45–46
Fraley, Maurice and Nina, carousel, *115*
Freyhold, K. F. Edmund von, *Easter Bunny, 39*
Friedenshase (Beuys), *14*
frieze, *52*; tile, *99*
Frost, Arthur Burdett, *Br'er Rabbit, 47*

G

game-pie dish, *102*
Glorification of the Virgin (Dürer), *70*
Goat, Hare, Wolf, and Leopard (Grassi), *69*
Gold Rab[b]it matchbook cover, *106*
Grassi, Giovannino de': *Goat, Hare, Wolf, and Leopard, 69*; *Magnificat, 34*
Grinstead, Rosie, quilt, *107*
Groening, Matt, *I'm Having the Weirdest Sense of Déjà Vu, 65*

H

handkerchief, *39*
handscroll, *66*
Hare (Dürer), *68*
Hare (Hoffmann), *74*
Hare, The (de la Mare), 55
Hare among Buds and Flowers, 80
Hare and Copper Cauldron (Chardin), *78*
Hare and the King of the Elephants at the Well of the Moon (Bidpai), *45*
Hare beneath a Tree (Hoffmann), *75*
Hare Hunt, 77
Hare Leaping over Moon (Yabuuchi), *2–3*
Hare on Bell on Portland-Stone Piers (Flanagan), *67*
Hares, Raurackl, and Squirrel (Hoefnagel), *73*
Hares Antiques, logo, *16*
Hare Seen from Above (Hoffmann), *71*
Harnett, W. M., *After the Hunt, 79*
Harper's cover, *84*
Harris, Joel Chandler, 45
Harvey (movie), 65
Herculaneum, wall painting, *42*
hieroglyphs, *23*
Hiroshige, Ando, *Sokkyo Kageboshi Zukushi, 111*
Hoefnagel, Joris, 69; *Hares, Raurackl, and Squirrel, 73*
Hoffmann, Hans, 69; *Hare, 74*; *Hare beneath a Tree, 75*; *Hare Seen from Above, 71*
Hummel, M. I., *Playmates, 19*
Humpen glass, *100*
hunting, 21–22, 76, 79, 100, *101*
hunting goblet, *101*
Hunting Scene, with Three Hounds Driving Two Hares into a Net, 76

I

Iliev, R., stamp design, *16*
I'm Having the Weirdest Sense of Déjà Vu (Groening), *65*
"In the Animals Court" (Twain), 52
Indians, North American, 32, 42, 45
Inkerka, tomb of, *23*

J

Jack-Rabbit (Nice), *43*
Jagyoku, Katsu, *Rabbits and Pine Trees in the Snow, 40–41*
jewelry, 91, *94, 95*

K

Kachikachi Yama, 58
Kalila wa Dimna, 69
Kimhi, David, *Army of Hares Besieging a Wolf in His Castle, 50*
Kornfeind, Jan, quilt design, *107*
Kunhardt, Dorothy, *Pat the Bunny, 109*

L

Last Judgment, The, 55
Lay of Aristotle, The, 31
Leigh, Janet, *112*
Leonardo da Vinci, 52
Leone, Angiolo, *San Domenico and San Francesco,* 56
Lepus americanus, 28
Lepus as Seen in the Sky (Sufi), 27
Lepus europaeus, 16
Lepus timidus, 28

M

Madonna and Child with Saint Catherine (Titian), *33*
Madonna with the Rabbit (Titian), 32
Mad Tea-Party, A (Rackham), *87*
Magician Performing a Hat Trick, 113
Magnificat (Grassi), *54*
majolica, *102, 103*
Manabozho, 42, 45
Mantegna, Andrea, 69
manuscripts, *21, 27, 34, 44, 45, 50, 51, 54, 66, 69, 72, 77*
March Hare (Tenniel), *86*
Mark, Mary Ellen, *Milos Forman,* 18
Mary, Queen of Scots, 76
matchbook cover, *106*
Mayan vase paintings, *24–25*
medicine bottle, *96*
Mennecy, snuffbox, *99*
Merriam, toys, *117*
Miró, Joan, *Still Life with Rabbit,* 81
Mixtec calendar, *25, 64*
Month of April (Cossa), *30*
Moon Goddess (Shoga), *21*
moon symbol, *21, 22, 24, 25, 39, 58, 64*
Moor, D. S., *Sovetskaya Repka,* 121
Morris, William, *Flora Tapestry,* 35
mosaics, *61, 62, 63*
Mounted Huntsman Attacking a Hare, 61
movies, 55, 65, *112, 122, 123*
Mr. and Mrs. Cottontail (Kornfeind), *107*
murals, *23, 42*
My Dream Is Yours (movie), *122, 123*

N

Nashe, Thomas, *Have with You to Saffron Walden,* 31
Nice, Don, *Jack-Rabbit,* 43
Nicholson, William: *Spring time,* 118; *Summer days,* 119
Nicolas of Modena, Master, frieze, 52
Noah Freeing the Animals from the Ark, 63

O

ojime, *90, 93*
Oswald the Lucky Rabbit (Disney), *122*

P

Paderborn Cathedral, *29*
Parrish, Maxfield, calendar illustration, *106*

Pat the Bunny (Kunhardt), 109
Peasant Holding Two Hares, A, 57
Penfield, Howard, *Harper's* cover, *84*
Piatti, Celestine, stamp design, *17*
Pinkney, Jerry, *Br'er Rabbit and the Tar Baby,* 48–49
Pisanello, Antonio: *Allegory of Luxury,* 31; *Study of a Hare,* 69
plate, *103*
Playboy logo, 31, *36*
Playmates (Hummel), *19*
Pliny the Elder, 76
Point, The (cartoon), *86*
postage stamps, 16, *17*
postcards, *38*
Potter, Beatrix: *Tale of Peter Rabbit,* 14, *108,* 109; *Tale of the Flopsy Bunnies,* 109
Pronolagus crassicaudatus, 28

Q

quilt, *107*

R

Rabbit (Cartier), *97*
Rabbit, Br'er, 45, *47, 48–49, 86*
Rabbit between Tall Grass (ojime), *93*
Rabbit in the Palm of a Hand, 58
Rabbit on the Wall, The (Burnet), 110
Rabbits (Dürer), *73*
Rabbits and Pine Trees in the Snow (Jagyoku), *40–41*
Rabbits in a Forest (Yabuuchi), *83*
Rabbits in a Meadow, 72
Rackham, Arthur: *Mad Tea-Party, 87; Why, Mary Ann, What Are You Doing Out There?,* 88
Rahman, Abd al-, *Book of Fixed Stars,* 27
Remus, Uncle, 22, 45
Rodgers, W. R., 79
Roger Rabbit, 64, *122*
rosette, *29*

S

San Domenico and San Francesco (Leone), 56
Saxon Idol of the Moon, A (Verstege), *21, 36*
Schaper, Johan, cup, *53*
screens, *40–41, 82*
Sense of Taste (tapestry), *6*
Shakespeare, William, 32, 85
Shoga, Takuma, *Moon Goddess,* 21
Smith, John Moyre, ceramic tile, *46*
snuffbox, *99*
Sokkyo Kageboshi Zukushi (Hiroshige), *111*
Southern Celestial Hemisphere, The (Dürer), *26*
Sovetskaya Repka (Moor), *121*
Spring time (Nicholson), *118*
Stanhope, Prince, *19*
Stewart, Jimmy, 65
Still Life with Rabbit (Miró), *81*
Studio 6 (Witschi), *64*
Study of a Hare (Pisanello), *69*
Sufi, Umar al-, *Lepus as Seen in the Sky,* 27
Suhayli, Answar-i-: *Animals in Council,* 12; *Elephants and Hares at the Well,* 44

Summer days (Nicholson), *119*
Summit, Rol and Jo, carousel, *114*
Swarovski, Daniel, crystal figures, *96*

T

Tale of Peter Rabbit, The (Potter), 14, *108,* 109
Tale of the Flopsy Bunnies, The (Potter), 109
Taming of the Shrew, The (Shakespeare), 32
tapestries, *6, 35, 60*
Taymouth Horae, 69
Tenniel, Sir John: *March Hare, 86; White Rabbit, 86*
Theatre Magazine cover, *37*
Thumper, 14, 64, 109, *123*
tiles, *46, 80, 99*
Titian: *Madonna and Child with Saint Catherine, 33; Madonna with the Rabbit,* 32
tomb paintings, *23, 57*
"Tortoise and the Hare, The" (tile), *46*
toys, *16, 116, 117*
trickster rabbits, 45–46, 64, 85
Triumphal Arch of Maximilian, The (Dürer), *73*
troop insignia, 14
Twain, Mark, "In the Animals Court," 52
Twohy, Mike, cartoon, *89*

U

Unclean Spirit, The, 51
Untitled (Cornell), *36*
Up n' Atom, 15

V

vegetable box, *15*
Velveteen Rabbit, The (Williams), 109, *118, 119*
Venus, 31–32
Verstege, R., *Saxon Idol of the Moon,* 21
Viking Ship and Creeping Things, 54

W

wall paintings, *23, 42*
Warner Bros., Bugs Bunny, 46, *47, 122*
Webster Co., bib clip, *107*
White Hare of Inaba, The, 58
White Rabbit, 52, 86
White Rabbit (Tenniel), *86*
Why, Mary Ann, What Are You Doing Out There? (Rackham), *88*
Williams, Margery, *The Velveteen Rabbit,* 109, *118, 119*
Witschi, Hans, *Studio 6,* 64
Woman with Rabbit Hat (Baskerville), *37*
Wordsworth, William, 85
Wraight, ojime, *90*

Y

Yabuuchi, Satoshi: *Hare Leaping over Moon, 2–3; Rabbits in a Forest,* 83

Photograph Credits

The author and publisher wish to thank the libraries, museums, galleries, and private collectors named in the picture captions for permitting the reproduction of works of art in their collections and for supplying the necessary photographs. Photographs from other sources are gratefully acknowledged below.

Acme Features Syndicate Reprint permission, Sheridan, Ohio: 65 (bottom). Alinari, Florence: 30. Art Resource, New York: 42 (top). From *Animals, Animals, Animals, A Collection of Great Animal Cartoons*, edited by George Booth, Gahan Wilson and Ron Wolin for the Cartoonist Guild [New York: Harper & Row 1979]: 89. Banques d'Images Textiles, Musée des Tissus de Lyon: 60. Jean Bernard, Aix en Provence, France: 55 (both). Bettmann Archive, New York: 19 (bottom), 112 (both), 113. Bildarchiv Preussischer Kulturbesitz, Berlin: 71, 74. Blue Lantern Studio, Seattle, Washington: 39 (top), 82, 124, jacket back 9 (top right). Jutta Brüdern, Braunschweig: 52, 91, 120. Cameraphoto, Venice: 56, 62, 63. Canali Photobank, Capriolo: 69 (top left). Mario Carrieri, Milan: 102 (top). James Dee/Paula Cooper Gallery, New York: 10–11. Richard Dennis Publications, Somerset: 46. Used by permission of Dial Books for Young Readers, a division of Penguin USA Inc.: 48–49. Used by permission of Doubleday, a division of Bantam Doubleday Dell Publishing Group, Inc.: 118, 119. Editions d'Art Albert Skira, Geneva: 76. Fabbrica di S. Pietro in Vaticano, Rome: 54. Takeshi Fujimori, Tokyo: 3. Yoshitoki Fukanaga, Tokyo: 83, jacket back (top left). Hirmer Fotoarchiv, Munich: 58 (middle). HNA-Archive, New York: 23 (bottom), 39 (bottom), 40–41, 66, 72, 86 (both), 108. Courtesy Nancy Hoffmann Gallery, New York: 43. William Holland/HNA-Archive, New York: 16 (bottom), 117 (both). Tom Jenkins, Dallas, Texas: 107 (bottom). Rollout Photography © Justin Kerr, New York: 24 (both), 25 (top). From John Layard, *The Lady of the Hare* [London: Faber & Faber, 1947]: 21 (bottom). From Hans van Lemmen, *Tiles: 1,000 Years of Architectural Decoration* [New York: Harry N. Abrams, Inc., 1993]: 80. Lichtbildwerkstätte Alpenland, Vienna: 31 (bottom), 68. Nicolo Maltese, Piazza Armerina: 61. Mary Ellen Mark/Library: 18. Nawrocki Stock Photo, Chicago, Illinois: 84. New York Public Library, Astor, Lenox and Tilden Foundation: 21 (top), 110. Wolfgang Noltenhans, Paderborn: 29. Reprinted by permission of Pantheon Books, a division of Random House, New York: 65 (bottom). John Parnell, New York: endpapers, 8–9, 38, 92. Pedone & Partners, New York: 19 (top). Photofest, New York: 65 (top), 122 (above right). © Playboy Enterprises, Chicago, Illinois: 36. PTT Stamp Printing Office, Bern: 17. R. M. N., Paris: jacket front [background], 6, 23 (top), 33, 69 (right). "The Arthur Rackham illustrations are reproduced with the kind permission of his family": 87, 88. Scala/Art Resource, New York: 34, 42, 94. Gerhard Schön, Munich: 28 (all). Gary Sinick, Oakland, California: 114, 115. R. Dahlquist/Super Stock, New York: jacket front (inset). Frederick Warne & Co., London: 109. The Walt Disney Company, Burbank, California: 14 (right), 122 (above left and below right), 123. Warner Bros. Consumer Products, Burbank, California: 47 (right). © Hans Witschi, New York: 64.

Illustration Copyrights

© Jennifer Bartlett/Paula Cooper Gallery, New York: 10–11. Joseph Beuys/VG-Bildkunst, Bonn/ARS, New York: 14. © The Joseph and Robert Cornell Memorial Foundation: 36. © 1983 Barry Flanagan: 67. Joan Miro/ADAGP, Paris/ARS, New York: 81. © 1976 Don Nice: 43. © by Universal City Studios, Inc. Courtesy of MCA Publishing Rights, a Division of MCA Inc. All Rights Reserved: 122 above left. © 1984 Hans Witschi: 64. © Satoshi Yabuuchi, Tokyo: 3, 83, jacket back (top left and borders), binding.

Acknowledgments

This book was inspired by Susan Jonas and Marilyn Nissenson. I am very grateful to my husband, Andrew, and my daughter Paula for all their help and patience. And special thanks to Colin O'Neill, Toni Monzon, Steve Dierkes, and Carl Gottlieb for their generous contributions.

Paul Gottlieb, Harriet Whelchel, Uta Hoffmann, Barbara Lyons, and Carol Robson provided invaluable support and assistance at Harry N. Abrams, Inc. And I would like to thank the staff of the Beverly Hills Library, the U.C.L.A. Library, and the Central Library of Los Angeles.